Herne Hill
Heritage Trail

Written and produced by
George Young, Margaret Wimble, Caroline Knapp,
Robert Holden, Jeffrey Doorn and John Brunton

With 47 illustrations,
including 10 line drawings by Don Bianco

First published in 2003 for
The Herne Hill Society
PO Box 27845
LONDON SE24 9XA
by
Local History Publications
316 Green Lane
Streatham
London SW16 3AS

ISBN 1 873520 46 8

INTRODUCTION

How often have we walked, cycled or driven through our neighbourhood and wondered what this grand building or that old shop-front used to be; who lived in the area in times past, or how that church or library came to be sited there? Perhaps we've pondered the significance of a plaque or marker; puzzled over a street sign or pub name; questioned how our favourite park came into being or what, if anything, once stood where our housing estate or school now stands.

The idea for this book was first discussed in 1999, when the Herne Hill Society decided to aim for publication of a walk around Herne Hill, to include all the places, buildings and objects of interest in our village. A provisional list of 60 items was drawn up; and an enthusiastic team formed to conduct research and write up each item. Initial discoveries led to further findings; and practice walks inevitably led to yet more sites and historical connections we could not very well leave out. The resulting list is double the original number!

Some readers may question the inclusion of certain items which appear on the fringes of our area. But then, Herne Hill does suffer from something of an identity crisis. Most of it is in SE24, but some bits stray into other post codes (or vice versa); we have indicated where addresses are SE5 or SE21. Another confusion-inducing fact is that we straddle two boroughs, Lambeth and Southwark.

When friends from other areas ask, "Herne Hill, where's that?" do we answer, "It's the central point of South London," or do we reply, "Well, it's not Dulwich or Brixton, but somewhere in between," or even, "No, *beyond* Camberwell."? So what is Herne Hill? The street of that name which extends from Denmark Hill to Herne Hill railway station? The station itself and surrounding area? The Lambeth ward, the boundaries of which have changed over the years? The road which runs from the top of Red Post Hill to Loughborough Junction? Well, all of these, and more.

But what is the origin of the name? The John Rocque map of 1746 shows the area as Island Green and Dulwich Hill, so that doesn't help. About 150 years earlier, Speede's map indicates King's Hill here, so perhaps James I had his eye on it. Some say the ancient streams, and particularly the River Effra, attracted large numbers of heron, and a hillock by the river came to be called Heron's Hill. Another interpretation of our curious name is 'hill by a nook of land,' deriving from the Old English *hyrne* (corner, angle) *hyll*. The first record of our place name seems to be 1798, Herne Hill possibly alluding to a field in Brixton c1490 called Le Herne. Sadly, we could find no connection with Herne the Hunter, the phantom who haunts Windsor Great Park; though he is but one manifestation of the Wild Huntsman myth of someone excessively fond of the chase who rashly makes a compact with a devilish stranger and is doomed to hunt forever. We trust that will not be the fate of our readers.

This book will be of interest to anyone who has lived, worked or studied in Herne Hill, or who has visited or passed through the area and is curious about its history, architecture or personalities. For those who wish to follow the walk, we have plotted one circular trail. As the complete circuit is rather long, you may prefer to cover a section at a time, starting and finishing where you wish and travelling in either direction. The maps give suggested ways to follow; and there is the option to go off-route to see something of interest which is technically outside our area. Whether you walk all or part of the route, or simply read about the sites with your feet up at home, we hope you will find the book useful and illuminating.

The writers have now formed the Local History Group within Herne Hill Society, to encourage interest in and to research the history of Herne Hill and the surrounding area; to record information and, where appropriate, to disseminate it to a wider public through publications, presentations, Newsletter articles etc. Our next project is a book on noteworthy people who have lived here or been associated with the area.

Mendelssohn's Song without Words, Op. 62 No. 6 'Spring Song'

Abbreviations

DCE - Dulwich College Estate
LBSCR - London, Brighton & South Coast Railway
LCC - London County Council
LCDR - London, Chatham & Dover Railway
GLC - Greater London Council
WW1; WW2 - First World War; Second World War

Transport and Practical Points

Numerous bus routes serve the Herne Hill area, as do suburban railway lines into four local stations. If flying in, there are direct rail links with Gatwick and Luton. Refreshment venues abound, to suit all tastes and budgets; Herne Hill is described in *Living South* as a "culinary oasis." We have tried to arrange the trail avoiding too many main road crossings. Certain sites are best viewed from across the road if there is not a safe crossing nearby; naturally, all roads should be crossed with great care. We hope you will enjoy learning about our village. If you discover something of interest which you think should be added to the trail, please let us know.

Acknowledgements

Our grateful thanks for the information and advice given by the following: John Brown, Graham Cannon, Mary Chorley, Annie Gelly, Derek Graydon, John Hopkins, Sid Hopkins, Patricia Jenkyns, Kevin Kelly, Sister Rose Lightbourne, Alan Piper, Peter Reeve, Doug Stephenson, Philip Spooner, Peter Whitworth, Bill Williams and Rev. Hettie Williams. Thanks also to the staff at Lambeth Archives, particularly Jon Newman, Sue MacKenzie and Nilufer York; Southwark Local History Studies Library, particularly Stephen Humphrey and Stephen Potter; London Metropolitan Archives; Peabody Estate Records, and Fire Brigade Records. Valuable contributions have also been made by Michael E Corby, financial donation; Damaris Dodds, indexing; Christopher Jordan, South London Gallery, and John Smallwood, processing illustrations.

 Published with the support of
Heritage Lottery Awards for All

LIST OF ILLUSTRATIONS

We have made every effort to trace copyright ownership
of illustrations; we apologise for any omission.

Herne Hill Heritage Trail

Map Index

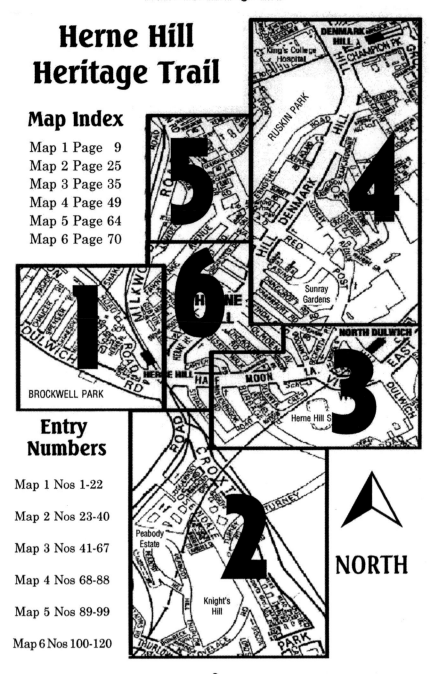

Entry Numbers

Map 1 Nos 1-22

Map 2 Nos 23-40

Map 3 Nos 41-67

Map 4 Nos 68-88

Map 5 Nos 89-99

Map 6 Nos 100-120

NORTH

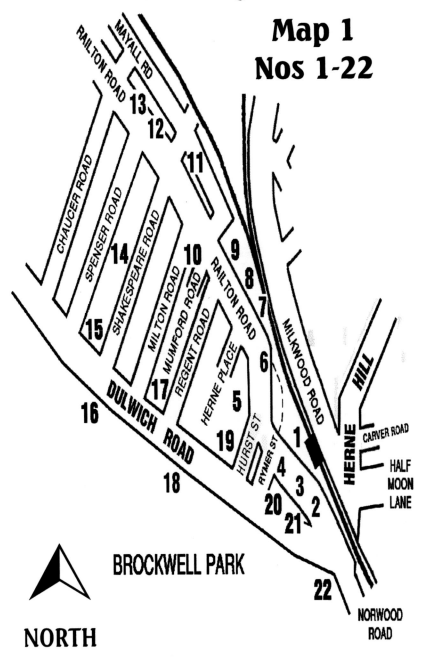

Map 1
Nos 1-22

NORTH

BROCKWELL PARK

HERNE HILL HERITAGE TRAIL

1 HERNE HILL STATION, Railton Road: The station was built for the LCDR on land owned by Thomas Vyse of the 'Abbey' (see **No. 114**), and opened to traffic on 25 August 1862. The architect was John Taylor Jr, and the railway engineers were Cubitt & Turner. The entrance building and platforms were designed to impress passengers. Cherry & Pevsner commented that the station was "a handsome group" being two storeys high, Gothic and of polychrome brick, with a taller tower for the water tank. The station entrance block was listed Grade II in 1999.

The first line to open from Herne Hill in 1862 was the route north to Elephant & Castle. This was extended over the Thames to Ludgate Hill (now Blackfriars) by 1864. The line north to Victoria via Brixton also opened in 1862, extending in 1863 south to Dulwich (later West Dulwich), Beckenham Junction and Bromley (later Bromley South). Finally, the line south to Tulse Hill opened in 1869, to connect with the LBSCR line from London Bridge to Wimbledon and Sutton. Steam trains were the order of the day. For many years in the 19th century, long distance trains from the coast divided here for Victoria and Holborn Viaduct. Electrification was completed in the 1920s.

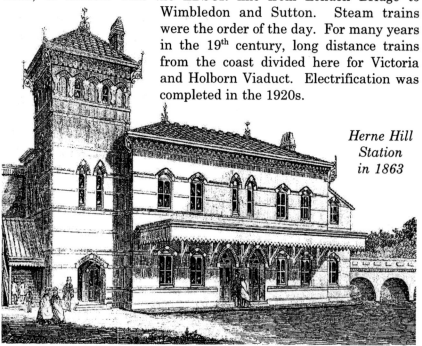

Herne Hill Station in 1863

Railton Road and Herne Hill Station c1921

2 RAILTON ROAD, formerly STATION ROAD: A road from the station was built to provide horse carriage access to the junction of Norwood Lane and Water Lane (now Norwood and Dulwich Roads) and Half Moon Lane. The road was unimaginatively called Station Road, as were many other roads next to stations. The 1871 census shows that most of the present shops had been built, although a few were unoccupied.

From 1884, Station Road was briefly called Bransby Road. In 1888 it became an extension of Railton Road, which had started from Atlantic Road, Brixton c1866-69. Railton Road was named in 1866 after Gregory Railton, a 16th century landowner in this area.

The longest serving shop here is the branch of J. Kennedy at No. 319, which opened in 1910, described as a 'ham & beef dealer'. Another long-standing shop was the branch of Home & Colonial Stores Ltd, tea & provisions dealers, at No. 218 from 1901-68.

3 Former CINEMA GRAND, 222 Railton Road: From 1900-13 the shop at 222 Railton Road was occupied by an estate agent and then by a hairdresser. It later became the entrance foyer to one of the earliest purpose-built cinemas in London. The cinema was built following the Cinematograph Act 1909, which had stipulated that projection equipment should be outside the auditorium and laid down regulations concerning emergency exits, number of seats and provision of aisles.

The Herne Hill Cinema was designed by Frank E Harris and constructed by Griggs and Son of Cubitt Town, at a cost of £5,000. It opened on 20 December 1913 with Edward Hardiman as manager. Some time afterwards, and certainly by 1921, its name was changed to the Cinema Grand.

It was a silent cinema with an orchestra pit, until the coming of sound in April 1930. In 1932, alterations were carried out to the designs of George Coles, the famous cinema architect, followed by the grand reopening on Boxing Day. Over the years thousands of people enjoyed seeing films here.

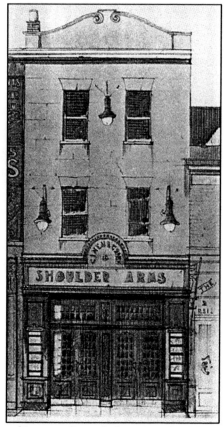

Cinema Grand showing the film Shoulder Arms c1918

In September 1953, the name was changed to the Pullman Cinema, and it closed on 27 June 1959 with *The Ladykillers* and *The Way to the Stars*.

It then became a popular bingo club, which finally closed in the autumn of 1986. In 1987, the Pullman Grand Theatre Project was set up with the aim of saving the building and converting it into a theatre. Although the Project was not successful in that respect, one benefit from the campaign was that over 1,000 people went on conducted tours of the building, and much information about its history was gathered. The auditorium in Dulwich Road was demolished in September 1999 and the foyer building has reverted to what it was before the cinema was built: a shop on the ground floor and living accommodation above. The parapet at the top of the building, which once carried the word GRAND, is the only reminder of its glorious past.

4 THE COMMERCIAL PUBLIC HOUSE, 210-212 Railton Road:

On the west side of Station Road at the time of the 1871 census were 1-3 Commercial Place (206-210 Railton Road) and 1-9 Commercial Terrace (214-230 Railton Road). In 1872 a beer retailer named Frederick Moles was in business between these two rows of shops. By 1876 the Commercial Hotel Public House had been built (later to be 212 Railton Road) with Frederick Moles still the landlord. The term 'hotel' was added to give the pub status. From 1898-1903, the landlord was William Shott Death.

In 1938 the pub was enlarged to its present size, incorporating 210 Railton Road, a hairdresser's shop. By the 1950s it had been taken over by a private company. The pub is now called The Commercial; the present owner is the Southside Pub Company.

London Welsh Rugby Football Club used to meet here in the 1970s and 80s, and they donated many different rugby shirts to the pub. At least 70 have been framed and are displayed on the walls.

5 198 GALLERY, 198 Railton Road: This art gallery was the brainchild of Zoë Lindsley-Thomas (1935-2002) and her partner, Noel Morgan. In 1988 they created the award-winning gallery, where are presented a wide variety of public exhibitions, designed to reflect the multicultural communities that make up Lambeth and the surrounding boroughs. The gallery is also active in arts education, with facilities and programmes particularly designed to engage the attention of disaffected young people from the area.

6 WEST PLACE and the FOOTPATH (Vyse's Alley): West Place was formed in the 1820s and comprised the present Railton Road from the former St Jude's School to the footpath starting at 239 Railton Road. Two roads off West Place were Regent Row (now Road) and Herne Place, largely built over by the Meath Estate c1966-68. The families living on West Place estate in the mid-19th century were working class; most of the men were gardeners or labourers.

The present footpath starts at 239 Railton Road and finishes in Dulwich Road next to the Brockwell Park Tavern. It was built for access to the new Herne Hill Station from Regent Row, Herne Place and West Place. Prior to the building of the station and railway (c1861-2) a much longer footpath existed from Coldharbour Lane/Atlantic Road in the north to The Half Moon public house in the south.

The north end of the path gradually became Railton Road when it was laid out c1866-69. The south end of the footpath was called Vyse's Alley, after Thomas Vyse, who had died in 1861.

7 Former STATIONMASTER'S HOUSE, 239 Railton Road: This

was built mid-1880s. From here station staff used to collect their wages each week. The Stationmaster had an excellent view of Herne Hill Station from an upstairs window. The house is now privately owned.

8 Former BRITANNIA PUB, 233 Railton Road: This was

originally built in the 1830s, and from 1860s-1930s it was the Britannia public house. The Census records of 1871 to 1891 and various Directories describe the occupier as a beer-house keeper and not a victualler or publican, so it was probably no more than an 'on' license, selling just beer (no spirits) for consumption on the premises. The house is now privately owned and has been converted into flats.

9 TEMPLE OF TRUTH PENTECOSTAL CHURCH, Railton Road:

The International Fellowship for Christ was established in England in the 1970s. Their church in Somerleyton Road, Brixton was the first church in the UK to be built by people from the West Indies; but they were obliged to move to their present address when Lambeth Council built a new housing estate on the original site in 1974. Their first pastor was Rev. A U Headlam. The present pastor (2003) is Rev. R Moore.

The buildings were converted from the former St Jude's C of E School and St Jude's Church Hall. The school was the single storey building on the right with lancet windows and grey brick. It was built in 1834, on land purchased by Mr & Mrs Thomas Simpson of Herne Hill, to provide Christian education for the infant poor,

St. Jude's School c1834

serving the West Place/Regent Row/Herne Place estate. In 1844 it became St Paul's Infant School and in 1869 came under the management of the newly formed St Jude's parish. In the centre is the tall two-storey brick extension to the school of 1894. The Church Hall is the two-storey gabled building on the left, built 1887.

The hall and school were severely damaged by bombing in 1940; the Rev. Arnold Hutton Hart-Davies (vicar 1949-58), a Canadian, was instrumental in getting them repaired and rebuilt. In 1973, St Jude's Primary School was relocated to a new building in Regent Road.

10 HAMILTON ARMS PUBLIC HOUSE, 128 Railton Road & Mumford Road:
The Hamilton Arms started out as a beer-house in the 1860s and was rebuilt in the 1930s by Watneys Brewery. The coat of arms on the sign outside does not appear to match any Hamilton family crest. Prior to 1937 Mumford Road had been a longer cul-de-sac called Hamilton Road; it was renamed for the Mumford family which lived in the area, including Catherine Mumford Booth of the Salvation Army.

11 **CINEMA POSTER BOARDS, Mayall Road:** In Mayall Road, on the side garden wall of 84 Shakespeare Road, there are two double poster boards with a single poster board between them. They would have carried posters for local cinemas; few such boards have survived. They are in such a dilapidated condition that they might not be there by the time you visit.

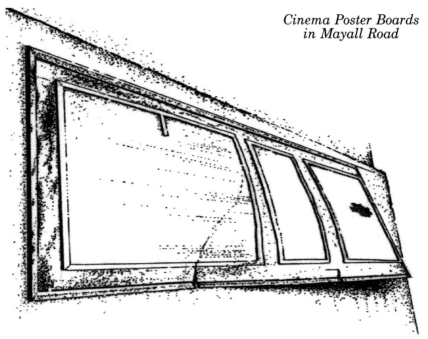

*Cinema Poster Boards
in Mayall Road*

12 **PLAQUE to ROTIMI FANE-KAYODE, 151 Railton Road:** The brass plaque is inscribed: 'Rotimi Fane-Kayode (1955-1989) Artist Lived Here'. The Nigerian born artist won renown with photographs depicting the male image, as well as artefacts and emblems of Yoruba culture. He was instrumental in setting up AUTOGRAPH, the Association of Black Photographers. Books include *Black Male/White Male* and a monograph produced with his partner Alex Hirst. Exhibitions of his work have been shown as far afield as the Castle, Cape Town and as near as the 198 Gallery, Herne Hill.

*Railton Road
Methodist Church*

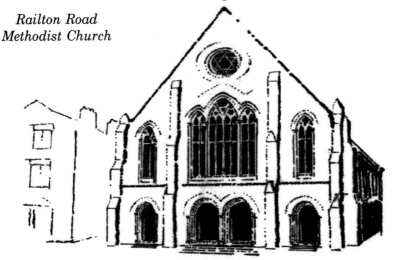

13 **RAILTON METHODIST CHURCH, Railton Road:** The present building dates from 1970 and was designed by architects Alistair McDonald & Partners. It has a hall and facilities for a youth club, play group and community centre. The first church was a temporary corrugated iron structure (these were known as 'tin chapels'), built 1869, situated between 25 and 27 Milton Road where Florence Villas now stand. As the surrounding population increased, the church attendance grew. A brick and stone church designed by R Cable was built in Railton Road on the site of a sandpit and opened in 1875. In 1940, a bomb fell on the corner of Spenser Road and severely damaged the church. The old building did not reopen until after WW2. It was demolished in 1968.

14 **POETS CORNER (Chaucer, Spenser, Shakespeare and Milton Roads):** Located between Dulwich and Railton Roads. Due to the literary street names, this area has been dubbed 'Poets Corner', especially by estate agents. It was designated a Conservation Area in 1999. The land was once Effra Farm, up to 1855, when it was purchased by the Westminster Freehold Land Society and the roads were laid out. Building was slow at first but accelerated in the 1860s after the building of Herne Hill and Brixton Stations.

The larger houses were built first. They had attics and basements to attract the middle classes, who would have had servants living in. The later houses were intended for those skilled working class families who could afford to move into better quality houses.

Before street numbering came to these roads in 1875, names would have been given to each detached house, to each pair of semi-detached villas and to each terrace.

Doulton Vase from the Woolley Collection

15 HOME of CHARLES WOOLLEY, 35 Dulwich Road:

Charles Woolley (1846-1922) lived from 1915 in this house, naming it Verulam after the city of St Albans, where his grandfather had been Mayor. A Lambeth Borough Councillor from 1900-12, Woolley represented Tulse Hill Ward, which then included Dulwich Road and Poets Corner; he was elected Alderman in 1906. Known as 'The Historian of Lambeth', he was especially interested in the borough's pottery manufacture. Having built an impressive collection of stoneware, he donated it to Lambeth in 1915 with the objective that it should form the basis for a museum. Just before his death, he urged the council to obtain permission from the LCC to use the soon to be vacant Brockwell House (then known, confusingly, as Brockwell Hall) for this purpose.

In 1899, Henry Wellcome (1853-1936) had established the Wellcome Physiological Research Laboratories (WPRL) in Brockwell Hall (i.e. House) and its stables accommodating 14 horses. WPRL conducted important scientific research, quality control and other commercial work. Here, A T Glenny (1882-1965) developed a system which greatly increased diphtheria anti-toxin production, and in 1915 built on Dr R A O'Brien's work by producing an anti-toxin protecting against tetanus and all three known gas-gangrene bacilli. The laboratories moved to Beckenham in 1922.

Despite the idea of obtaining it for conversion into a Lambeth Museum, Brockwell House was demolished; and the Woolley Collection, largely unseen, remains in the care of Lambeth Archives.

16 Former ST JUDE'S CHURCH, Dulwich Road:

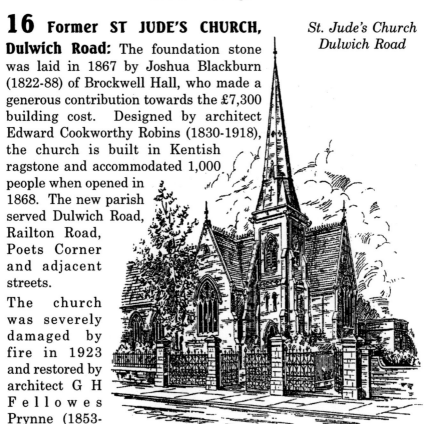

*St. Jude's Church
Dulwich Road*

The foundation stone was laid in 1867 by Joshua Blackburn (1822-88) of Brockwell Hall, who made a generous contribution towards the £7,300 building cost. Designed by architect Edward Cookworthy Robins (1830-1918), the church is built in Kentish ragstone and accommodated 1,000 people when opened in 1868. The new parish served Dulwich Road, Railton Road, Poets Corner and adjacent streets.

The church was severely damaged by fire in 1923 and restored by architect G H Fellowes Prynne (1853-1927). During WW2 it suffered extensive bomb damage; and in 1952 a chapel was made from part of the east aisle, while the rest of the church remained disused. In 1975, the congregation moved out to the former St Jude's School; and the church was declared redundant in 1978. It has since been used as a warehouse for office furniture.

17 PRINCE REGENT PUBLIC HOUSE, 69 Dulwich Road:

Situated on the corner of Regent Row (now Road), it was built in the 1820s when the present Dulwich Road was part of Water Lane, and the River Effra flowed above ground alongside. The pub is the second oldest in SE24 after The Half Moon. The present building dates from about the 1860s and is handsomely fitted with many original features including fine upstairs rooms and some old cellars.

18 BROCKWELL LIDO, Brockwell Park, Dulwich Road: The LCC Parks Department built the Lido, an open-air swimming pool, in Brockwell Park in 1937. G P Trentham was the builder and Harry Arnold Rowbotham (1879-1954) the architect. Rowbotham designed many buildings in LCC parks. The cost was £24,150 paid by Lambeth and £2000 by the LCC. The Mayor of Lambeth, Alderman E A Mills JP, opened the Lido on 10 July 1937.

London led in the provision of lidos in urban areas. There was increasing concern for the nation's health in the 1930s, partly caused by the high incidence of rickets and tuberculosis (TB), and a growing awareness of the importance of a balanced diet. Cod liver oil was supplied to meet diet deficiency. Increased exposure to sunlight was being promoted to stimulate the formation of vitamin D in the body. Also by this time, shorter working hours were providing better opportunities for healthy leisure pursuits.

Over the years, the use of lidos declined as funding for repairs and maintenance became a problem. Recently (2001-2), Evian, the French bottled water company, sponsored the Lido, briefly re-christening it 'Evian Lido'. Brockwell Lido is the only lido in the UK that is not subsidised. It offers yoga, meditation classes and some workshops for under-fives (Whippersnappers). There are also workshops and play schemes for children and adults. The lido has a poolside cafe. At present (2003), the future of the Lido is being discussed; the staff and users of this great facility are determined to keep it going.

Dulwich Rd Methodist Church

19 SITE of 89 DULWICH ROAD and METHODIST CHURCH: This is now a grassed area, located between Regent Road and Hurst Street in front of the 18-storey Park View House and opposite the Lido car park. William Booth (1829-1912), founder of the Salvation Army in 1865, met Catherine Mumford (1829-90) in 1851, when as a Methodist lay-preacher he came to her chapel, a branch of the United Methodist Free Church. They married in 1855.

The chapel had started in 1836 in the house in Water Lane of Mr James Fosbery, a postman. The house became 89 Dulwich Road in 1875. When Fosbery died there in 1884, it was demolished; a temporary iron building was erected on the site for the Dulwich Road Methodist Church, opening in 1887. In 1910, a permanent church was built; it was in use until the mid-1960s, when the present blocks of flats were built by Lambeth Council.

20 BROCKWELL PARK TAVERN, 133 Dulwich Road: This was built in the 1860s as the Railway Tavern public house, address 21 Herne Terrace, becoming 133 Dulwich Road in 1875. It was renamed the Brockwell Park Hotel c1892 when Brockwell Park opened. About 1936, the pub was enlarged to incorporate 131 Dulwich Road, the shop next door.

21 SITE of CINEMA GRAND AUDITORIUM, 135 Dulwich Road: The first building on this site was Lawn House, the Stationmaster's house up to the 1880s. It is believed that there next came a laundry, which was demolished in 1913 to make way for the Cinema Grand auditorium. The back wall of the cinema and the passageway from the entrance can still be seen. The alleyway between Dulwich Road and Railton Road was known as Brockwell Passage. The block of flats with two shops on the ground floor was built in 2000.

22 BROCKWELL PARK & BROCKWELL HALL: The jewel in the crown of Herne Hill is Brockwell Park, the 50 hectares (120 acres) of which make it undoubtedly the grandest of Lambeth's open spaces. From the perimeter the ground slopes gently upwards to the twin hills of Brockwell Hill and Tulse Hill, from the tops of which there are splendid views.

Until 1807, the whole of Tulse Hill and Brockwell Park formed a single estate, known in the 13th century as the Manor of Bodley, Upgrove and Scarlettes. Between 1352 and 1537 it was owned by St Thomas's Hospital, then a monastic establishment in Southwark. After Henry VIII seized the monastic estates, the land changed hands several times, and by the 1650s was owned by the Tulse family. The original Brockwell Hall stood near Norwood Road,

Thomas Lynn Bristowe Memorial Fountain

roughly opposite the present Rosendale Road. An account of a court hearing held there in 1563 describes it as 'Brockalle'; other Tudor records refer to Brockholds, and the road that ran past it as Brockholle Lane.

In 1807 the estate was split in two; the western part was eventually developed as Tulse Hill. In the next few years most of the eastern part was bought by John Blades, a wealthy City glass merchant, who demolished the old Hall and built a new house on top of the hill. Most of the original fields were laid out as the private park of the new Hall. Some of the houses in Brixton Water Lane were built for estate staff. In between, Clarence Lodge was built in 1825 where the BMX track is today. In 1828 work started on a street of houses, Brockwell Terrace, on the site of the Lido; but development came to a halt with John Blades' death in 1829.

Blades' grandson, Joshua Blackburn, inherited the estate on his mother's death in 1860, and building soon resumed to take advantage of the opening of Herne Hill Station in 1862. Brockwell House was added between Clarence Lodge and the Hall, and a line of houses was built along the south side of Dulwich Road. Joshua contributed to the cost of the new St Jude's Church,

Brockwell Hall 1820

doubtless with one eye on further development with the church at the centre of a new neighbourhood; but in his later years he was confined to a lunatic asylum, and died in 1888.

In that year the Lambeth Vestry obtained consent to make a new public park on the east side of Brixton Hill. When it became apparent that the Brockwell estate would come on the market, Thomas Lynn Bristowe (1833-92) of Denmark Hill, first MP for Norwood, led a campaign to buy the larger and more attractive site. The LCC bought 78 acres (33 hectares) in 1891, with contributions from local authorities and the community. The formal opening by Lord Rosebery took place on 6 June 1892, but tragically Mr Bristowe collapsed and died at the close of the ceremony. A drinking fountain was erected to his memory in 1893, and stood near the Herne Hill entrance until 1958.

After the park opened, efforts continued to obtain the remainder of the estate. Another 3.5 acres were bought in 1895 to provide access from Brixton. J J B Blackburn, Joshua's son, died in 1898; the LCC bought the remaining 43 acres from his trustees in 1901. This extension was opened formally in 1903; but until the leases expired on the four remaining houses, only about half was actually available. The last house was demolished in 1923, and its site incorporated into the park. Management of the park passed from the LCC to the GLC, and then in 1970 to Lambeth Council, who are the custodians today.

Suggested route - (Allow at least one hour): Herne Hill Gate to Lido, with miniature railway track on right; uphill, passing Redgra football pitches and BMX track, bowling green and tennis courts. Over hill into valley. Here, a tributary of the Effra once flowed freely but has now been tamed to feed the two man-made ponds in the small wooded area. At bottom, pass ponds and a larger one built as a swimming pool but now the home of fish, ducks and geese. Miniature village.

The Walled Garden, or Old English Garden, was originally a kitchen garden to Brockwell Hall; it is now a flower garden containing: a well, small pond, aged mulberry tree, wooden shelter, sundial (fixed to the brickwork behind an old wisteria). The Garden's brick walls are early 19th century and were listed Grade II in 1951. Outside is a shelter, sometimes called the Summer House, with a blank pediment and octagonal wooden columns. Path to cast-iron Clock Tower (a smaller version of the one in front of Victoria Station), presented 1897 by Charles Ernest Tritton (1845-1918), MP for Norwood 1892-1906. It was listed Grade II in 1981. The park office comprises a former coach house and stable block, plus surrounding brick walls, all listed Grade II.

Brockwell Park Clock Tower

Brockwell Hall was built 1811-13 as a gentleman's suburban villa, designed by D R Roper. It was listed Grade II* in 1975 and restored after serious fire damage in 1990. The interior has some period features; one room is painted with murals by Henry Strachey c1897 (not usually open to view). The house is now used as offices and has long featured a park restaurant. Meandering path downhill towards Norwood Road gate. Norwood Lodge is an original gate-lodge to the former Blades estate, built early 19th century. Nearby is a stone horse trough, provided by the Metropolitan Drinking Fountain & Cattle Trough Association, moved here from the bottom of Rosendale Road. *Return to Herne Hill gate.*

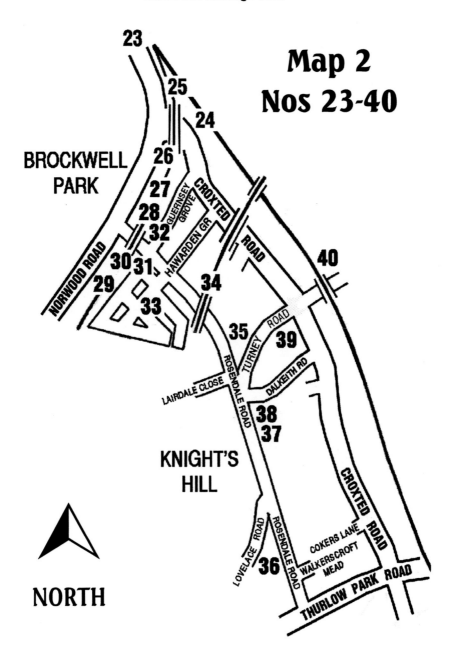

Map 2
Nos 23-40

BROCKWELL
PARK

KNIGHT'S
HILL

NORTH

23 **SHOPS, 11-87 Norwood Road:** These are single storey lockup shops, built c1925, overlooking Brockwell Park. One exception is the two-storey house at No. 81 dated 1894. The shops were built to serve the growing population of the area and also possibly to hide the view of the railway arches. Shops already existed in Railton Road, Dulwich Road and Half Moon Lane.

Croxted Lane c1850

24 **CROXTED ROAD:** Crockestrete, a crooked or winding street, was on a 14th century pilgrims' route to Canterbury. Another explanation of the name is that the road was made up with broken crockery or tiles from old kilns in the area. It appears on Rocque's map of 1746 as Crookesed or Crocksed Lane. Later it became Croxted Lane and finally Croxted Road in 1873, soon after the arrival of the railways. It runs from Norwood Road to the junction with Park Hall Road and then becomes South Croxted Road. The houses at the northern end of the road were built c1900.

25 **RAILWAY BRIDGE, Croxted Road (near Norwood Road):**
Opened 1869 by the LCDR, it conveys the railway between Herne
Hill and Tulse Hill. The land is owned by the DCE, and the
Governors insisted on an ornamental cast-iron facade and railings
both sides, with badges denoting the letters 'AC' (Alleyn's College).
Charles Barry Jr (1823-1900) designed the facades, which are
independent of the steel beams carrying the railway. The circular
columns are not structural but now purely decorative.

26 **LOGO of the FISHER
BOOKBINDING CO. 89-91
Norwood Road:** The Fisher
Bookbinding Company
occupied this site on the
corner of Croxted Road
from 1902-69. The
kingfisher logo and the
Grecian pilasters are
attractive features of
this building. From
1969 it was the offices of
the Inner London
Probation Service and later a
printing company, Matro
Thomas Jenkins Ltd, which closed
in the late-1990s.

27 **103, 103a-d NORWOOD ROAD:** These five terraced houses,
built 1956-7, are now part of the Brockwell Park Conservation Area.
They are town houses typical of the 1950s and are on the site of
Stanhope Lodge, a large detached early Victorian house, home from
c1885-1909 of Francis Fearon, a solicitor. Mr Fearon and his sons
were keen mountaineers and members of the Alpine Club. In 1902
two of his sons climbed the Wetterhorn in Switzerland in hazardous
conditions. Tragically, when they reached the summit they were
killed by lightning. The Fearons were parishioners of St Paul's,
Herne Hill; there is a brass tablet in the church commemorating the
sons, Henry Charles Digby Fearon and Robert Burton Fearon.

28 **119-121 NORWOOD ROAD:** This pair of late Regency Grade II listed houses on the corner of Norwood Road and Rosendale Road were built on part of what was Brockwell Green Farm. The farm was purchased by Lord Thurlow in 1785, and 27 acres were sold in 1826 to John Prince of Leadenhall Street, a slop-seller (slop: ready-made or cheap clothes).

The houses were built soon after 1826. The front elevations are of "a Grecian design reflecting the influence of the late 18th century French architect, Ledoux" (Claude-Nicholas Ledoux, 1736-1806). They were known as Nos. 1 and 2 The Limes, Norwood Lane, up to 1882 when the present addresses were assigned. Both houses were in residential use until the 1920s.

After that, No. 119 became a small factory/office for, at different times, a tea dealer, printer, gown maker, a garage and a builders. In 1955 it opened as the One One Nine Club, becoming the Bon-Bonne Club discotheque in 1971.

No. 121 became the home of Hommel Pharmaceuticals 1926-62, and then Multipax Chemicals Ltd 1963-77. The Bon-Bonne Club has used both houses since 1980. There is an empty stable block in the grounds next to No. 119.

Swiss Cottage

29 **SWISS COTTAGE, 155 Norwood Road:** This curious black and white house in the style of an alpine chalet dates from c1850. It is in the Brockwell Park Conservation Area, which covers this side of Norwood Road from here to Croxted Road.

Thomas Burrell, a brick manufacturer employing 13 men, 8 boys and 2 women, lived here at the time of the 1861 census. In 1871, another brick maker, Henry King, lived here and employed 49 men and 9 boys. His brick fields were located south of Trinity Rise.

Alpine houses were a fashion of the mid-19th century. The Swiss Cottage in Finchley Road NW3 was a tavern built c1830 (rebuilt after WW2). At the junction of Poplar Walk and Herne Hill there used to be a pair of houses called Swiss Cottages, 14-16 Herne Hill, which were demolished c1910.

30 BRICK RAILWAY BRIDGE, Rosendale Road: Located near the

junction of Norwood Road and Rosendale Road, it was opened in 1869 to connect the line between Herne Hill and Tulse Hill stations. Cherry & Pevsner describe it as "three-arched with heavily modelled red and cream brickwork." The central arch is elliptical. It was listed Grade II in 1981.

31 Former MILK DEPOT, 279 Rosendale Road: From 1906-81

this now rather dilapidated building next to the railway bridge was the Express Dairy depot and shop. Attractive features are the four small circular openings at high level with white surrounds and blue painted bricks. There were stables for horse-drawn milk carts at the back. The depot is now used as a store.

32 NEW TESTAMENT CHURCH OF GOD, Guernsey Grove: The

New Testament Church was founded 1866 in the USA, where it is known as The Church of God; it has branches in 160 countries. The British branch, known as The New Testament Church of God, was founded in September 1953 by Rev. Dr Oliver A Leyseight at YMCA Hall, Waterloo Road, Wolverhampton. It is now the largest black-led Pentecostal Church in the UK, with a hundred churches in England, four in Scotland and three in Northern Ireland and with a membership of 9,500. The church building in Guernsey Grove was purchased in 1975.

It was built originally as St John the Evangelist Church (C of E), a daughter church of Holy Trinity Church in Trinity Rise SW2. St John's started in a small wooden shack in Croxted Road when the Peabody Estate was built 1901-05. The congregation increased, so a larger but temporary iron church ('tin chapel') was built in Guernsey

Grove. In June 1911, the foundation stone to the present building was laid. The architect was Leonard Martin (1869-1935), formerly of the Treadwell & Martin partnership. The 'tin chapel' was moved to Abersoch in North Wales.

33 PEABODY ESTATE,

Rosendale Road: Building began in 1901 on the site of Thompson's brickworks, of four blocks containing 144 flats. The architect was Henry Astly Darbishire (1825-99); the builder was William Cubitt & Co. In 1905, 82 cottages were built, and in 1907-8 a further 64 were added, all to the designs of William Edmund Wallis (c1851-1912), a former assistant to Darbishire. The tenants' hall was built in 1913 and is an unusual feature of the Trust's work. The War Memorial was erected by the tenants to 35 men from the Estate who lost their lives in WW1. The whole estate is now a Conservation Area.

War Memorial, Peabody Estate

The flats were built for working class people. In order to qualify for a home, applicants had to be born in London, within ten miles of Charing Cross. Prospective tenants were interviewed: married couples (proof of marriage was required), with a good moral background, were in the majority. Tenants were inspected annually; if found to be satisfactory, one week's free rent was given. Each landing had a tap at one end and a lavatory at the other. Tenants were responsible for cleaning the landings. A superintendent, who lived rent free, was responsible for maintenance of the building. He and his wife supervised bathing by tenants in the communal baths. The policy of screening tenants of good background and behaviour remains to this day.

George Peabody (1795-1869) was an American, born in Massachusetts. He was a self-made man who made a great fortune as a merchant and banker. During his lifetime, he gave away a fortune for philanthropic purposes. He came to London in 1837 and, appalled at the dreadful housing conditions of the working poor, funded a number of housing estates in London, the first in Spitalfields (1864). He was regarded as a hero and given the Freedom of the City of London, a great honour for an American. He was also offered a Knighthood, which he declined. When he died, his body lay in state in Westminster Abbey before being taken home for burial in his hometown, re-named Peabody in his honour.

34 SECOND RAILWAY BRIDGE, Rosendale Road: This bridge,

south of the Peabody Estate, was built 1866-68 for the LBSCR, linking North Dulwich and Tulse Hill stations. As at **No. 25,** the ornamental facades were by Charles Barry Jr and were required by the DCE, the landowners. The north facade incorporates four metal panels each showing three badges. The badge on the left is that of the railway company; in the centre the letters 'AC' denote Alleyn's College with the date '1866', and on the right is the badge of DCE. The circular columns now have no structural function.

There was a third railway bridge, now demolished, immediately south of this bridge. From c1894-1970 it served the Knights Hill Goods and Coal Depot next to the Tulse Hill railway tunnel entrance. The depot site is now the Lairdale housing estate built by Lambeth Council.

35 ROSENDALE PRIMARY SCHOOL, Rosendale & Turney Road

SE21: The site for the school was purchased in 1894. At the time, people living in the area objected to the proposed building on the grounds that the values of their properties would depreciate. They also pointed out there was no need for a school as no poor children lived in the area. A temporary iron structure, erected in 1897, was replaced by the present Junior school built by the School Board for London in 1900. The architect was Thomas Jerram Bailey (1844-1910); the building was listed Grade II in 1981. The classrooms are large; in the days before central heating, fires were lit in each one.

The Infant school was built by the LCC and opened in 1908. The Schoolkeeper's House in Turney Road is a curious building with unusual buttresses.

36 ALL SAINTS CHURCH, Rosendale Road SE21: *Although it appears to be off route, the church is well worth a detour.* This Grade I listed building, now sadly a shell, was severely damaged by fire on 9 June 2000. English Heritage had recently completed major restoration work on the roof (1998). The crypt survived the fire and services are now held there. The church had previously been damaged by bombing in 1944 and restored in 1952. All Saints was an impressive brick building based on French medieval cathedral designs, with very fine interior and stained glass windows. The architect, G H Fellowes Prynne, was a pupil of G E Street, who designed St Paul's Herne Hill. The church was built 1888-91, to accommodate 1400 people; the entire cost of £16,000 was raised by parishioners and local residents. It was dedicated on All Saints' Eve, 31 October 1891.

A new church is to be built within the shell of the old church. Among the fundraisers is Jim Davidson of Brockwell Art Services, Railton Road; he cycled 800 miles of the pilgrims' route from Lourdes to Santiago de Compostela, for sponsorship funds.

All Saints Church in 1891, the year it was built.

Benchmark Stone in Rosendale Road

37 **BENCHMARK STONE, Rosendale Road SE21:** Located between 234 Rosendale Road and the Playing Fields, this white stone, marked 'Alleyn's College Dulwich 1908,' shows the benchmark symbol indicating a known level (124.5' at that time) above mean sea level. These once commonplace symbols used to be chiselled onto permanent features, such as bridge parapets and church plinths.

38 **234-240 ROSENDALE ROAD SE21:** These four semi-detached houses were built for the Ideal Home Exhibition in 1924, and people were brought by bus from Earls Court to view them. The architect's name was Skinner.

39 **CROXTED ROAD SE21, junction with Turney Road:** John Ruskin knew Croxted Lane, as it was then called, from his childhood. In *Modern Painters,* written 1843-60, he says "there, my mother and I used to gather the first buds of the hawthorn; and there, in after years, I used to walk in summer shadows...." He often came this way from his home on visits to Dulwich Picture Gallery.

Ruskin wrote: "The slender rivulet, boasting little of its brightness...yet fed purely enough by the rain and morning dew, here trickled...through the long grass beneath the hedges, and expanded itself, where it might, into moderately clear and deep pools...."

Up to the 1860s the main course of the Effra ran parallel to Croxted Lane from Thurlow Park Road to just south of Turney Road. From here there is a slight upward slope on Croxted Road; the river turned east to meander across what is now Turney Road, the sports grounds and Burbage Road to Half Moon Lane, where it turned west towards Herne Hill.

In the 1880s while staying at 28 Herne Hill, Ruskin wrote despairingly of Croxted Road: "I walked through what was once a country lane, between the hostelry of the Half-moon at the bottom of Herne Hill, and the secluded College of Dulwich...no existing terms of language known to me are enough to describe the forms of filth, and modes of ruin, that varied themselves along the course of Croxted Lane. The fields on each side of it are now mostly dug up for building...."

This would refer to the detached and semi-detached villas, built c1875, from Park Hall Road to just south of Turney Road.

40 RAILWAY BRIDGE, Turney Road SE21: This bridge was built 1863 by the LCDR to connect Herne Hill and West Dulwich stations. It was renovated in 2003. Similar to the railway bridge over Croxted Road, it has the same cast-iron facades and railings, as required, designed by Charles Barry Jr. The west elevation has lost the centre section of its balustrade; original balustrading and a plaque showing the date 1863 can best be seen from the south-east side. There is a height limit of 4.1m (13'6").

Charles Barry Jr.

Map 3
Nos 41-67

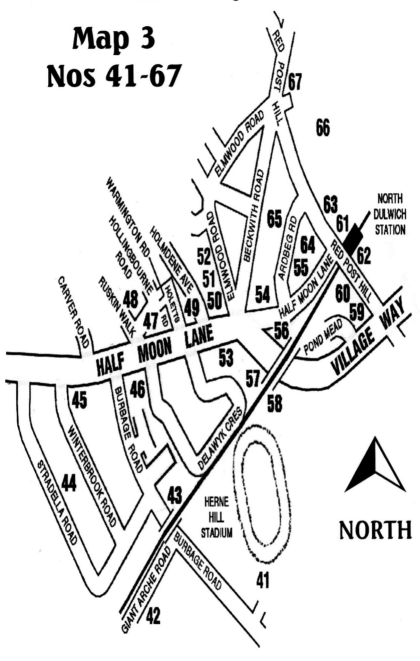

NORTH

41 HERNE HILL CYCLE STADIUM, 104 Burbage Road:

To build this stadium, The London County Athletics Ground Ltd. was floated in 1892 by George Lacy Hillier (1856-1941), a stockbroker and a leading amateur racing cyclist. In 1894, it is said, 20,000 people came to watch the principal races. The stadium became the leading venue for competitive cycling, and from 1926 world records were set here. It played host to the 1908 and 1948 Olympic Cycling events and to legendary names from cycling throughout the years, such as Beryl Burton, Fausto Coppi, Reg Harris, Daniel Morelon, Marty Nothstein and Florian Rousseau.

BRIXTON, LEWISHAM & LONDON BICYCLE CLUBS'
(AFFILIATED TO THE N.C.U.)

JOINT RACE MEETING

London County Grounds, Burbage Road, Herne Hill, S.E.,

SATURDAY, JULY 8th, 1893,
COMMENCING AT 3.30 P.M.

Herne Hill Cycle Stadium Poster 1893

From 1892 to the 1990s there was an athletic (cinder) track, used primarily by the Herne Hill Harriers up to 1937. Crystal Palace Football Club played at the Stadium from 1915 to 1918. King's College Medical School used the grass area for rugby football. A new cycle track was laid out in 1993 and the gradient increased to 26 degrees. A veterans' cycle club show is held each year on the first weekend in June. Everything from pennyfarthings and boneshakers to recumbent cycles are on show. Herne Hill Stadium is perhaps the oldest cycle stadium in the world.

42 DULWICH SPORTS CLUB, Giant Arches Road, off Burbage Road:

The Dulwich Sports Club is a combination of six sports clubs run as a Limited Company for cricket, tennis, squash, running, croquet and hockey.

The Dulwich Cricket Club is the oldest club meeting here and was founded in 1867 when the Camberwell Music Society decided to form the Aeolian Cricket Club. It moved to Turney Road in 1885 and in 1888 merged with the neighbouring Lennox CC to form the Dulwich CC. The club has had many successes including the Surrey Championship in 1974, 1975 and 1976 and the final of the National Club Knockout at Lord's, where they lost to Scarborough. The touring West Indies side played here in 1928 (it was a draw). Many Dulwich players went on to play for their country. The entrance to the ground is south of the railway bridge on the west side. Concrete medallions on the brick railway arches leading to the ground show the date 1866 and initials 'AC' for Alleyn's College.

43 RAILWAY BRIDGE, Burbage Road: This is the tallest bridge in SE24 and was built 1866-68 for the LBSCR, linking North Dulwich and Tulse Hill stations. As elsewhere, it has the required ornamental facades by Charles Barry Jr. The only metal badges to be seen are those of Alleyn's College on each brick pier, both sides at high level. The circular columns now have no structural function.

44 SPRINGFIELD ESTATE, Winterbrook & Stradella Roads: This estate, now part of a conservation area, is bounded by Half Moon Lane in the north, Burbage Road in the east and railway lines in the south and west. It once contained a large mansion called Springfield, built in the 1830s, designed by Charles Barry (1795-1860), surveyor to the DCE. From 1859-89 it was inhabited by John Gregory Crace (1809-89), of the prestigious firm of Crace and Son, architectural decorators. Their work included the decoration of the Royal Pavilion at Brighton for George IV. J G Crace was the fourth generation of the firm; he worked on the decoration of Chatsworth House, Knebworth House, the Houses of Parliament (with A W N Pugin), Windsor Castle, the International Exhibition of 1862 and Longleat House. His son, John Diblee Crace (1838-1919) carried on the business until 1899; when he retired the firm was wound up.

The mansion was demolished in 1889. The DCE then built Stradella Road, Winterbrook Road and part of Burbage Road, and lined them with the present houses, built to attract a growing population of the middle class, mostly employed in the City of London. It was hoped that they would send their sons to Dulwich College.

45 HERNE HILL BAPTIST CHURCH, Half Moon Lane: In 1897, a small group of Baptists met for services in a railway arch near Loughborough Junction. A site was subsequently acquired in Winterbrook Road to build a church and a church hall. The church hall was built in 1899, to the designs of Charles Barry Jr, his very last commission. In 1904 the church was built to the design of J William Stevens. The style was described by English Heritage as "Non-conformist Art Nouveau-cum-Gothic Revival" when it was listed Grade II. It has a bell tower, given by A J Tucker from Onaway, 173 Half Moon Lane. This was the first non-conformist church on the DCE.

*Ancient Elm Bole
in Half Moon Lane*

46 SITE of ANCIENT ELM BOLE, Half Moon Lane: For over four centuries a massive elm tree stood in the vicinity of the present 48-50 Half Moon Lane. With a hollow trunk measuring 20-36' in diameter, it was said to afford sitting room for 12 people. Local tradition holds that Queen Elizabeth I rested beneath its branches after a royal barge trip up the Effra. By the early 20th century it was held together by strong chains; and the top of the trunk was trimmed in 1928 in hopes of preserving it "for another half century or so." However, the legendary tree was pulled down in the early 1980s to make way for Dulwich Mead.

47 PLAQUE to RICHARD CHURCH, 2 Warmington Road: The poet, novelist, essayist Richard Church (1893-1972) lived here 1905-12. He attended Dulwich Hamlet School and became a civil servant. He wrote affectionately of his time in Herne Hill and Dulwich in his three-volume autobiographical work: *Over the Bridge, The Golden Sovereign* and *The Voyage Home.*

Sam King, Mayor of Southwark 1983-4, also lived in this house. He came here from Jamaica in 1948 and moved to this address c1959, staying about 30 years.

48 TWO BOUNDARY MARKERS, Nos. 1 and 3 Warmington Road:

The plaque on the side wall to 1 Warmington Road reads 'CP 1889', denoting Camberwell Parish 1889. From here the Camberwell/Lambeth parish boundary used to follow Ruskin Walk downhill and then change direction along Warmington Road. The plaque on the front wall to No. 3 reads 'CP 1888' and indicates another direction change, eastwards. Similar plaques along the old Camberwell boundary can be found in Cormont Road and Thurlow Park Road.

The marking of boundaries goes back a thousand years. Before reliable maps (e.g. ordnance survey) and good documentation, it was important for individuals to know the extent of the parish boundaries, as this determined the number of households upon which rates could be set to pay for road maintenance and poor law, and tithes for the upkeep of the parish church. Over the centuries, many boundary disputes arose and some took years to resolve. Knowledge of boundary limits used to be kept afresh by the annual custom of 'beating the bounds' during Rogation Week. Most of these 'bounds' were situated along streams, roads and hedgerows, usually where they changed direction. By the mid-19th century, there were no doubtful boundaries left, and the markers and posts are now largely forgotten.

On the formation of the Metropolitan Boroughs of Camberwell and Lambeth in 1900, these old markers became redundant; the present borough boundary runs along the middle of Croxted Road, Norwood Road, Herne Hill (the road) and Denmark Hill.

49 THE OLD DAIRY, 127 Half Moon Lane: This was Welford

Surrey Dairies from 1908-20; R. Higgs & Sons Dairies, 1921-29 and United Dairies, 1930-62. Since 1963 the shop has been a newsagent. The rear building, which can be seen from Howletts Road, was a dairy where cows are said to have been kept. It has a hayloft, a tiny fireplace and a butler's sink. Milk would have been sold direct from the dairy. Pasteurisation and bottling of milk became compulsory in the 1930s. In 1960 the rear building was briefly occupied by builders and later used as a china store. From 1996-99 it was the Half Moon studio of etchers Sonia Rollo and Susie Perring. The building was converted into housing in 2003.

50 THE OLD BAKERY, 139 Half Moon Lane: The first mention

of a bakery here was in 1909, with James Swan as the baker, and it remained a bakery until 1988. It was originally all one business; the bread was baked at the rear and sold in the shop at the front. The front is now a dry cleaners; the rear is M. H. Associates, Chartered Surveyors, the entrance to which is in Holmdene Avenue.

51 CLASSICAL STRUCTURE/FOLLY, 149 Half Moon Lane: *Enter*

by the pavement in Half Moon Lane and view from a distance as it is on private property. The folly is a small Greek temple-like structure comprising four Doric columns, about two metres high. It may have been a feature that existed in the garden of the former house at 149 Half Moon Lane, or moved here when the flats were built in the 1960s. A high-explosive bomb destroyed the house in 1940.

Also of interest on this site are two large stones lying flat, possibly two of the seven boundary stones that marked out 'Howletts Acre', a narrow meadow of 1 acre and 17 perches (about 0.45 hectare), occupied now by the houses at the SE corner of Holmdene Avenue. Howletts Acre was given to pay the 'poor of Camberwell' by Sir Edmond Bowyer, a Camberwell landowner, in his will of 1626. The Trustees sold the land in 1859 in exchange for annuities. Howletts Acre is commemorated by Howletts Road.

Classical Structure

52 'WGT's WALL' INSCRIPTION, 74 Elmwood Road: The

Southwark Council flats, 78 to 106 Elmwood Road, are on the site of a large house, formerly 149 Half Moon Lane (sign still visible on adjacent brick pier). From c1910-25 it was the home of Walter George Tucker, an American (d 1959). It has been suggested that he was a 'drugs baron' of the day, although this cannot be substantiated; he was more likely to have been connected with his father's patent medicine business.

From c1928 the old house was used for a private school called Glenshee House, run by three sisters, the Misses H M, M M & M J Green and Miss P I Lynn. In 1940 a landmine damaged the house, and the school carried on across the road at 68 Half Moon Lane until 1943. The brick boundary wall fronting the flats in Elmwood Road is part of the original boundary wall to the old house.

53 JAMES BLACK FOUNDATION, 68 Half Moon Lane: This

world-renowned organisation was established in 1988 by Nobel prize-winner Sir James Black FRS (1924-2002). The foundation has close links with King's College and with its School of Medicine and Dentistry. In the superbly equipped biomedical laboratories here, using many innovative techniques and original approaches to research, scientists work to find new candidates for possible drugs that can be used to treat disease.

On this site were 62 to 68 Half Moon Lane, four detached houses built in the 19th century. No. 62, called Northfield, was occupied by Edwyn Barker from the 1880s-1930s; his wife ran a school here from the 1890s. The Bishop of Southwark 1942-58, Rt Rev. Bertram Fitzgerald Simpson (1883-1971) spent his retirement here.

No. 64 was in residential use until 1949 and No. 66 (still standing) until 1960.

No. 68 became St Marylebone School for Orphan Girls 1923-34 and later Glenshee School 1940-42. King's College London, Department of Botany (later known as Dept. of Plant Sciences) took over No. 68 in 1950, and gradually expanded, taking over Nos. 62 to 66.

Methodist Church, Half Moon Lane, c1905

54 HERNE HILL METHODIST CHURCH HALL, Half Moon Lane:

The church hall was designed by architect Maurice Bristow (1914-83) and built in 1953. The old church of 1900 was badly damaged by a WW2 bomb; and a block of flats, Wesley Court, was built on the site in 1980. The congregation amalgamated with the United Reform Church in Red Post Hill in 1985 and the hall is now used as a centre for a variety of activities.

55 ONAWAY, 173 Half Moon Lane: This large, rambling house

was built in 1901, probably named for a character referred to in the epic poem *The Song of Hiawatha* by Henry Wadsworth Longfellow (1807-82). The poem had been very successfully set to music by Samuel Coleridge-Taylor in 1900. An American named Augustus Quackenbush Tucker lived here until his death in 1917. The house was used for his patent medicine business until c1925, and was converted into flats in 1927. Onaway and the houses in Ardbeg Road were built on the site of a mansion named Dulwich House, home of the Lett family, who were North Lambeth timber merchants (not Letts of diary fame). They owned the land roughly bounded by Danecroft Road, Red Post Hill, Herne Hill, Ruskin Walk and Half Moon Lane. The last resident, Urania Lett, died in 1890. Dulwich House was then demolished, and the surrounding area sold and laid out in a coherent plan over the next 20 years with streets with smart late Victorian and Edwardian houses.

56 WHITEFORD STUDIO, 70 Half Moon Lane and 43 Village

Way: An artist's studio with huge dormer windows above a copper roof, built 1998 to the design of architects Cullum & Nightingale for Kate Whiteford (b Glasgow 1952). Some of her works are displayed at the Scottish National Gallery.

57 GRAFTON REGAL DANCE CENTRE, 7 Village Way SE21:

Grafton Hall was built in 1910 for functions, possibly by Charles Day (1855-1924) of 66 Half Moon Lane. He was its secretary 1912-20. The Grafton Lawn Tennis Club was based here for a time (secretary also Charles Day). The address was originally East Dulwich Grove, changing to 7 Village Way in 1925.

During WW2 in 1942 the LCC Meals Service opened a British Restaurant here. This was part of a campaign by the Ministry of Food to save fuel on cooking at home and to educate the public in sensible eating. Food rationing had begun in 1940 and virtually all foodstuffs were rationed. One British Restaurant in London in 1942 served roast beef, two veg., treacle pudding, bread & butter and coffee for 11d (about 4½p); others were described as selling 'belly fodder'. The population was told that it was part of our war effort - our patriotic duty - to eat at the centres, and it was also a chance to meet other people. A lot was learned about the science of food from wartime experiences, and food services owed much to British Restaurants. Rationing was gradually eased from 1948 and finally abolished in 1954.

After the war the Hall was used again for functions; since 1975 it has been a dance centre.

58 RAILWAY BRIDGE, Village Way SE21: This bridge was built

1866-68 for the LBSCR, connecting North Dulwich and Tulse Hill stations. It is similar to the second Rosendale Road bridge, with identical cast-iron facade and railings and badge panels, as required by DCE, designed by Charles Barry Jr. There is a height limit of 4.4m (14'3") and double-decker buses cannot pass under this bridge.

Lyndenhurst in 1929

59 LYNDENHURST, 19 Village Way SE21: This early 18th century house is the oldest in the area. In reddish brick with red brick dressings, it features a central timber doorcase with Doric columns, and a mansard roof with dormer windows behind a parapet. The single storey projection to right of the door is a later addition. The house was listed Grade II in 1954.

60 MARCHIONESS PLAQUE, outside 1-9 Red Post Hill SE21: The small plaque can be found on a brick pier of the back garden wall of Lyndenhurst, to the left of a small grass area in front of 1-9 Red Post Hill. It states that the trees and plants here are in memory of two people who died in the *Marchioness* riverboat disaster of August 1989. The disaster occurred at night on the River Thames, between Southwark Bridge and Cannon Street Railway Bridge, when the sand dredger, *Bowbelle* (80m long), struck the pleasure cruiser, *Marchioness* (26m long), with over 100 partygoers on board. Fifty-one people drowned.

61 **NORTH DULWICH STATION, Red Post Hill SE21:** This was built 1866-68, designed in Jacobean Revival Style for the LBSCR by Charles Barry Jr, architect and surveyor to DCE. The station is largely unchanged and, together with the platforms and attached road bridge, was listed Grade II in 1987. The station opened 1 October 1868 and initially served the line connecting London Bridge and Peckham Rye to Tulse Hill, Streatham, Wimbledon and Sutton. Murals by William Penn School/Dulwich High School students and art teachers adorn the platforms: 'The Journey Up' (1994) in terracotta, and 'Our Natural Environment' (1996), a painting, on platform 1; 'The Journey Down' (1995), and 'Our Built Environment' (1997), paintings on platform 2.

On the bridge opposite the station entrance can be seen four identical cast-iron painted panels fixed to the brick parapets. Each panel comprises three badges: the railway company (LBSCR); 'AC' (Alleyn's College) 1866, and DCE badge. North Dulwich station was the setting for an early feature film: *A Railway Tragedy* (1904) made by the Gaumont Studio of Champion Hill.

62 **TRADITIONAL RED GPO TELEPHONE BOX, North Dulwich Station:** This red cast-iron kiosk (or 'box') is one of the few that remain after a purge to remove them by BT in the 1980s, a rare example still in use outside the West End of London. It is a type K6, produced in 1935, and was listed Grade II in 1987. The design for the red kiosk was by the architect Sir Giles Gilbert Scott (1880-1960). The top of the kiosk was copied from the Desenfans mausoleum (1814) by Sir John Soane (1753-1837) at Dulwich Picture Gallery.

Milestone on Red Post Hill

63 **MILESTONE outside 20 Red Post Hill:** John Ruskin would have known this milestone when he described Herne Hill as "a rustic eminence four miles south of the Standard at Cornhill; of which the leafy seclusion remains...unchanged to this day" (1885). The milestone, just half a mile south of Ruskin's former Herne Hill home, actually states '4½ miles south of the Standard.' This milestone, which was listed Grade II in 1972, has been here since c1772, when Thomas Treslove, Surveyor of Roads, set up many of these throughout the country. Distances from the City of London were measured from The Standard, an old water conduit, in Cornhill.

Red Post Hill is so named after an 18th century signpost, painted red, at the top of the hill, pointing towards Dulwich.

64 **BOUNDARY STONE outside 11 Red Post Hill:** A white stone marker set into brickwork reads 'C P 1870' indicating a change in direction of the Camberwell/Lambeth boundary. The boundary ran near Half Moon Lane, and then from here turned up Red Post Hill towards Sunray Gardens. On the formation of the Metropolitan Boroughs of Camberwell and Lambeth in 1900, this area became all Camberwell, but the boundary markers were never removed.

65 **HOME of THE LUPINO FAMILY, 33 Ardbeg Road:** Members of the famous theatrical family, the Lupinos, lived here from 1917-29, including Stanley Lupino (1894-1942), actor, pantomime artist, writer and popular star of musical comedies, and his wife, Constance O'Shea (1891-1959), singer and dancer (stage name Connie Emerald).

Their daughter Ida Lupino (1918-95) was born in this house. A child star in Britain, she and her sister, fellow actress Rita (b1921), went to Hollywood, where Ida became a glamorous screen star, producer and writer, television actress and pioneering film and television director, whose success paved the way for future women directors.

66 THE CHARTER SCHOOL, former WILLIAM PENN SCHOOL, Red Post Hill:

The school can be seen from the end of the driveway opposite Ardbeg Road. The Charter School is the only secondary school in SE24. It was formed in 1999 after a campaign for a co-educational community secondary school in this part of the London Borough of Southwark. It opened for local children in September 2000 with four forms of 11 year olds and it is planned to have a 6th form by 2005.

Striding Man

The buildings opened in 1958 for the William Penn Secondary School for Boys, a comprehensive high school formed in 1947 by the combination of two Peckham schools, following the LCC's plan to implement the Education Act of 1944. It was proposed that new secondary schools would accommodate between 1250 to 2000 pupils.

William Penn School was designed to take 1250 boys of all abilities, but by 1958, due to the post-war increase in births (the 'bulge'), it had 1600. In the 1950s and 60s the school had a flourishing 6th form, many clubs, an orchestra, cadets and football, rugby and cricket teams. It was run on a 'house' system with houses named after local worthies Bessemer, Ruskin, Goldsmith, Paxton, Wilson and Faraday.

A sculpture called 'Striding Man' was erected in the school grounds in 1961. The sculptor was Oliffe Richmond (1919-77), who came from Tasmania in 1948 and later worked with Henry Moore (1898-1986). The sculpture was listed Grade II in 1998 and is considered one of the outstanding pieces commissioned by the LCC in the period 1945-65.

By the 1990s the number of pupils at William Penn had decreased, exam results were poor, single-sex schools were out of favour and too few parents were willing to send their sons there. The school was re-named Dulwich High School for Boys in 1996, but the name change had little effect and the school was closed in 1998. Now transformed architecturally and educationally, the Charter School is proving a great success.

67 ST FAITH'S CHURCH & HALL, Sunray Avenue: At the
beginning of the 20th century, the population of North Dulwich was increasing, and a church for that part of the parish of St Paul's Herne Hill was needed. The site was made available by the DCE, and the parish hall was built in 1909 at a cost of £2,944, to serve as a temporary place of worship.

The architects were Greenaway and Newberry. Cherry & Pevsner described the building as "progressive for its date" and noted the large dormered slate roof and "low arched west window between stumpy turrets" (one containing a bell, which has been transferred to the church). In 1986, £450,000 was raised and the hall was transformed into a community centre, now used by over 20 organisations.

St Faith's Church was designed by architects David Nye and Partners and built 1956-7 at a cost of £36,709. Much of the cost was met by War Damage Commission payments to churches in the diocese which were destroyed but never rebuilt after WW2. The vicar, Kenneth McIsaac (1900-56), played a key role in the planning of the church. Laurence Lee, Head of the Department of Stained Glass at the Royal College of Art, made all eight of the church windows. His other works include windows for Coventry Cathedral. The sculpture (the Calvary) on the external west wall is by Ivor Livi.

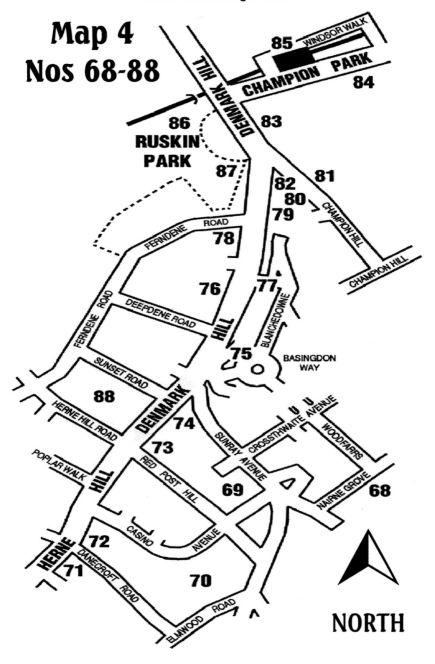

Map 4
Nos 68-88

68 BESSEMER GRANGE PRIMARY SCHOOL, Dylways SE5:

Pevsner described this as "a good example of the most recent (i.e. 1950s) work of the LCC Architects Department." It was built to serve the new Denmark Hill Estate on the site of the former homes of Henry Bessemer and John Ruskin, and is named after the Grange, the house Bessemer built for his daughter and son-in-law. The school occupies the site of the artificial lake that Bessemer built in the grounds. Note the English oak tree in the playground, over a hundred years old.

Opposite the school and next to 15 Nairne Grove there is a small Nature Reserve owned by the school. It is used for teaching purposes and as an educational resource.

69 SUNRAY ESTATE, Sunray Avenue, Red Post Hill and Casino Avenue: The Sunray Estate (now aka Casino Estate) was built 1920-22 by the Office of Works under Sir Frank Devis as a reply to Lloyd George's call for 'Homes fit for Heroes'. It comprises 292 dwellings, mainly two-storey houses, and was widely admired for the quality of design and speed of building. The estate has two distinct halves.

The estate *north-east* of Red Post Hill is on the site of the grounds of Dulwich Hill House, a large mansion, later 169 Denmark Hill, which was the home of Matthias Attwood (1780-1851) and his son Matthias Wolverley Attwood (c1807-65), both bankers and MPs, from the 1840s. Thomas Lynn Bristowe, MP and founder of Brockwell Park, lived there in the 1880s. Sunray Avenue was laid out across the grounds in 1894 by the Red Post Hill Land Company, which was formed to build 50 private semi-detached and detached houses. However, only a few were built at the top of Sunray Avenue, and the remainder of Sunray Avenue land was left unused for the next 18 years.

The estate *south-west* of Red Post Hill was occupied by a mansion called Casino (or Casina) House, and the name is now commemorated by Casino Avenue. Casino is Italian for 'Country House'. The house was built in 1796 and it is thought that the architect was John Nash (1752-1835). Humphrey Repton (1752-1818) designed the 15 acres (6 hectares) of gardens and it is known that Nash was collaborating with Repton at that time. It was built for Richard Shaw (c1755-1816), the solicitor who acted for Warren Hastings (1732-1818) at the spectacular show-trial at Westminster Hall, 1788-95, when Parliament impeached Hastings on charges of mismanagement of funds when he was Governor-General of Bengal 1774-85. Hastings had brought £40,000 back from India and by coincidence that was the same amount that Shaw spent on building Casino House. Shaw is buried in Dulwich Burial Ground; his large, impressive tomb can be seen from Court Lane.

About 1830, Casino House was occupied by Joseph Bonaparte (1768-1844), elder brother of Napoleon and uncle of Napoleon III. From the 1830s the lease was held by William Stone (c1793-1857), a silk broker, and later by his son, William Henry Stone (1834-96), MP and Magistrate for Surrey and Hants. The last resident, from c1880, was William Sutton Gover (1822-94), founder and managing director of the British Equitable Assurance Company. After Gover died the house remained empty until 1906 when it was demolished. The precise location of Casino House was at the top of the hill near the main road (Herne Hill) and immediately opposite Poplar Walk.

Casino House, Dulwich Hill

70 SUNRAY GARDENS, Red Post Hill:

70 SUNRAY GARDENS, Red Post Hill: This attractive little public park was created from the water gardens of Casino House when the Sunray Estate was built. It was first called Casino Open Space, changing to its present name in 1923. The original estate of around 15 acres (6 hectares) was landscaped by Humphrey Repton with gardens around the house and sloping paddocks leading to the lake at the bottom of the hill. The Park is a rare surviving example of Repton's work.

The lake was an important feature of the garden; it was reduced in size when the park was created, and made shallow and given shelving banks after a small girl nearly drowned in the 1930s and was rescued by a local postman. An early print shows that the original owner used the lake for fishing.

The park has tennis courts and a playground and is a focal point for the local community who come to see the varied wildlife. The outline of the original gardens still forms the street frontage of Sunray Gardens today. It is thanks to the persistence of the Friends of Sunray Gardens, formed 1997, that the park was refurbished in 2002 with grants from Southwark Council Environmental Improvement Plan totalling £220,000.

71 HOME of SAX ROHMER (1886-1959), 51 Herne Hill:

Rohmer was the celebrated author of mystery crime stories, most famously those featuring the sinister and dastardly Dr Fu Manchu, written from 1913 until a few months before his death, and adapted for radio, TV and film. He and his wife lived in this house with his father, who paid the deposit and shared the mortgage, from 1910-20. Sax's real name was Arthur Henry Ward; he was also known as Arthur Sarsfield Ward. The GLC erected a Blue Plaque in 1985 on the Danecroft Road side of the house.

Sax Rohmer

72 SITE of ELHANAN BICKNELL's HOUSE, Danecroft Road:

The top of Danecroft Road, built c1902, is the approximate site of a large mansion called Carlton House, home of Elhanan Bicknell (1788-1861) from 1819-61. He was a partner in Langton & Bicknell, oil merchants of Elephant & Castle, specialising in refining spermaceti oil. During his lifetime he built up a magnificent collection of paintings, all by British artists such as Gainsborough, Turner, Roberts and Landseer. He became well acquainted with the artists; and his son, Henry Sanford Bicknell (1817-80), married David Robert's daughter, Christine. After his death, 122 of his paintings were sold at Christies in 1862 for £75,000, a record sum at that time.

73 HERNE HILL UNITED CHURCH & HALL, Denmark Hill/Red

Post Hill: The present church was opened in 1960. Because of poor ground conditions it is a lightweight structure built on piled foundations. The architect was ✝ Ernest W Banfield.

The original church, with its hall, was built in 1904 as Herne Hill Congregational Church, but the building suffered from ground settlement. It was severely damaged by a WW2 bomb in 1944. The hall remains and is still in use; the Herne Hill Society holds its monthly meetings here. The Congregational Church became the United Reform Church in 1972, and in 1985 combined with the Methodists to become the Herne Hill United Church.

Herne Hill Congregational Church 1923

74 BOUNDARY POST outside KNOX HOUSE, 169 Denmark Hill

SE5: The small block of flats, Knox House, was built c1963 and named after Dr Alexander Campbell White Knox (c1899-1961) whose surgery was here at the former 169 Denmark Hill from 1927-61. The boundary post, dated 1870, marked the change in direction of the parish boundary between Camberwell and Lambeth. From this spot the boundary went along Denmark Hill from Herne Hill and cut across land towards Champion Hill. The boundaries were changed in 1900. The small raised figure on the post represents St Giles (d c700), patron saint of 'lepers, beggars and cripples'. The parish church of Camberwell bears his name. Identical posts along the old Camberwell boundary can be found in Myatts Fields, Thurlow Park Road, Gipsy Hill, Crystal Palace Parade, Sydenham Hill and One Tree Hill.

75 SITE of SIR HENRY BESSEMER's two HOUSES, near Swinburne Court, Denmark Hill SE5:

Sir Henry Bessemer (1813-98) is well known for his invention in the 1850s of the 'Bessemer Converter', a process that blew air through molten pig iron, removing impurities such as carbon and sulphur, to produce quality malleable steel in large quantities. His invention was to revolutionise steel production, introducing an era of cheap, mass-produced steel, enabling great improvements to gun-making, ship plate, railways and civil engineering.

Sir Henry Bessemer

His other inventions included the manufacture of bronze powder and gold paint in 1840, both of which were very successful; also, in the 1870s, somewhat less successfully, a swinging saloon for seagoing ships to reduce seasickness. Much of his wealth was derived from royalties he received from his 114 patents, connected mainly with the iron and steel industry.

In 1863 he moved to the 40 acre (17 hectare) estate in Denmark Hill, where he passed many years of busy leisure. He demolished the existing mansion and built a new one to the designs of Charles Barry Jr, calling it Bessemer House. A few years later he built an adjacent house, The Grange, in mock Elizabethan style, for his daughter Elizabeth (1834-1915) and her husband William Wright (1827-1908). The two houses became 165 and 167 Denmark Hill in 1883. Other features of the estate were a lake, a model farm, an underground cavern and an observatory housing the

Hillcrest Lodge

then second largest telescope in the world. Hillcrest Lodge, near the current junction of Sunray Avenue and Denmark Hill, served both this and the Dulwich Hill House estate; it was demolished c1961.

From 1910-22, Sir William Vestey (1859-1940) leased 165 Denmark Hill. His business was cold storage (Union Cold Storage Company) and shipping (Blue Star Line). During WW1, he turned No. 165 over to the War Office as a hospital.

Bessemer's House

No. 167 became a private residential hotel in 1910, run by Edwin Bartlett, and in 1923 both Nos. 165 & 167 were run as a hotel by William Wilson. From 1933-47 Nos. 163, 165 & 167 were the Ruskin Manor Hotel.

The mansions were demolished in 1947 to make way for the present houses and blocks of flats erected by the Metropolitan Borough of Camberwell.

76 HOME of FREDDIE MILLS (1919-65), 186 Denmark Hill SE5 (opposite Shaftesbury Court 25-36):
This popular and 'gutsy' boxer became world light-heavyweight champion in 1948 when he defeated Gus Lesnevitch at White City. This was at a time when British world champions were rare. He lost the title to Joey Maxim in 1950. In 1948 he married at Herne Hill Methodist Church and moved to 186 Denmark Hill (called Joggi Villa), where he lived until his death. During the 1950s and 60s he was well known and respected for his charity work.

77 SITE of JOHN RUSKIN's HOUSE, Denmark Hill SE5 (near Cross Court, Blanchedowne and Shaftesbury Court):
John Ruskin (1819-1900), the influential art critic and friend of J M W Turner, lived in a house owned by his father on this site. It was a large Georgian house of three storeys with a porticoed front door, standing in 7 acres (3 hectares) of ground. Ruskin's father, John James Ruskin (1785-1864), a prosperous wine merchant and partner in the firm of Ruskin, Telford & Domecq, sought a large house, fitting for his status.

Ruskin's House on Denmark Hill

The Ruskins moved here from 28 Herne Hill in 1842. It was here that Ruskin senior was able to display his large collection of watercolours, mainly by Turner, Prout and Roberts, to stock his cellar with wine and to entertain many literary, artistic and influential people. Some of Ruskin junior's short-lived marriage (1848-54) to Effie Gray was spent here.

When John senior died, John junior inherited the property, and his cousin, Joan Agnew (1845-1924), came to live here as companion to his mother, Mrs Margaret Ruskin. After his mother died in 1871, Ruskin sold the house to Walter Druce (1833-1905), a distiller, and moved to Brantwood, his house near Coniston in the Lake District. The house was numbered 163 Denmark Hill in 1883. In 1900 the house and grounds became wholly in Camberwell; before then, the Camberwell/Lambeth boundary ran through the rear garden, the house itself being in Lambeth. In c1907 the house became a private residential hotel. In 1933, together with Bessemer's former houses next door, Nos. 165 & 167, it become a larger hotel called Ruskin Manor. This was demolished in 1947 to make way for the present blocks of flats and houses erected by the Metropolitan Borough of Camberwell: see coat of arms over the central entrance to each block.

78 164 DENMARK HILL: A large, white mid-19th century house still remaining although much altered. Up to 1938 it was 'Heatherlea', 180 Denmark Hill.

79 FOX ON THE HILL PUBLIC HOUSE, 149 Denmark Hill, SE5:

This was opened in 1954 on the site of 149, 151 and 153 Denmark Hill. It replaced the Fox-*under*-the-Hill, which had stood at 119 Denmark Hill on the south corner with Champion Park, dating from the 18th century when it was an entertainment resort known as Little Denmark Hall. It is believed to have been the scene of many hunting meets with foxhounds. Nearby Dog Kennel Lane (now Hill) gives credence to this, though the name may be a corruption of the Canel (or de Canels) family who lived in Dulwich in the 15th century. Denmark Hill was so named after Prince George of Denmark (1653-1708), consort of Queen Anne, whose hunting lodge stood where Little Denmark Hall was later built.

Fox-under-the-Hill 1925

In the early 19th century the Dulwich Patrol started from the Fox-under-the-Hill and proceeded up Denmark Hill to Casino House turning down Red Post Hill to Dulwich. The patrols were 'watchmen' employed to deter burglars and robbers prior to the creation of the Metropolitan Police in 1829. The Fox-under-the-Hill was destroyed by a land mine in 1941; however, the licensee Frank Bailey and his wife sheltered safely in the basement. Bailey carried on in a temporary building and later in the new pub.

80 HOME of JOHN BELCHER, RA, 2 Champion Hill SE5 *(next to Fox on the Hill)*: Belcher (1841-1913) was President of RIBA 1904-06. Among his architectural achievements are the Mappin & Webb premises, Poultry (1871, demolished 1994); the Catholic Apostolic Church, Camberwell New Road (1875), damaged in WW2, now St Mary's Greek Orthodox Cathedral; offices of Institute of Chartered Accountants, Moorgate (1892); Colchester Town Hall (1898); Electra House, Finsbury Pavement (1902), now City of London University; The Ashton Memorial, Lancaster (1906); Whiteley's stores, Bayswater (1910), and many other public and domestic buildings.

Belcher designed the house in 1885 (see date on rainwater hopper) and called it Redholm. He lived there until he died. When the Fox on the Hill was built, the house was used as the public bar for a time. The house was severely damaged in the storm of 1987, when the three tall chimney stacks were blown down and dislodged large areas of the roof tiles. Two of the stacks were rebuilt to a reduced height. The house was listed Grade II in 1988, and was converted into flats c1999. Note the 1806 Dulwich Manor boundary stone in front of the house.

81 CHAMPION HILL, SE5: *A pleasant offshoot of this Trail,* Champion Hill extends south from Denmark Hill, passing Belcher's House, and at the road T-junction turns east to Dog Kennel Hill and west to Green Dale. First developed in the 1820s and 30s for wealthy merchants and businessmen, its large mansions were similar to those on Herne Hill and Denmark Hill. However, in Champion Hill the residents organised their own road maintenance and street lighting, and erected entrance gates to the road.

A few of the mansions still remain, such as Champion Lodge (No. 29) and Durleston Manor (No. 23). The Platanes (No. 12) has been enlarged and provides student accommodation for King's College, London. Over time, the other mansions have been demolished and replaced with housing estates or flats, such as Ruskin Park House, The Hamlet, Cleve Hall Estate, Anderton Close and Langford Green. Three Dulwich Manor boundary stones and one Camberwell Parish marker can be found in Champion Hill.

82 SITE of SUPPOSED PLAGUE PIT, Denmark Hill/Champion Hill SE5: The triangular plot of land (car park and grassed area) in front of the Fox on the Hill and bounded by Denmark Hill and Champion Hill is traditionally known as the 'plague pit,' and sometimes as the 'upper triangle.' While there is no evidence of any plague victims' burials, no one has ever built on this site.

Note across the road the red telephone kiosk, which we visit and describe at No. 87.

83 PIRIE CLOSE, Denmark Hill SE5: Sir John Pirie (1781-1851),

baronet, lived in a house near here in Champion Hill. Pirie, a merchant and ship owner, became Lord Mayor of London in 1841. Also near here, behind the present Kwik-Fit Centre, was a row of houses called De Crespigny Terrace. Samuel Prout (1783-1852), a watercolour painter, lived at No. 5 from 1844. He was a friend of the Ruskins of Denmark Hill. John Ruskin said in later life, "Prout ... always remains fresh to me; sometimes I tire somewhat of Turner but never of Prout."

84 WILLIAM BOOTH COLLEGE, Champion Park SE5: Built as a

memorial to their founder William Booth and opened in 1929, this college (originally to be called a 'garrison') was founded for the exclusive purpose of training students (cadets) for full-time service as officers in the Salvation Army. Those who graduate from the college provide constant revitalisation and re-staffing of the Salvation Army for both its evangelical and social work.

This Grade II listed building was designed by Sir Giles Gilbert Scott, architect of Liverpool Anglican Cathedral, Battersea Power Station, Waterloo Bridge and the red GPO telephone boxes. From a distance, the building with its 58m (190') high tower somewhat resembles Scott's Bankside Power Station (now Tate Modern) built in the late 1950s. The two bronze statues at the front of the building in Champion Park are of William Booth and Catherine Booth, by George Edward Wade (1853-1933).

85 DENMARK HILL STATION, Windsor Walk/Champion Park

SE5: The station was built 1864-66 jointly by LBSCR and LCDR and opened for traffic on 13 August 1866. English Heritage described the building as "high Victorian Gothic" when it was listed Grade II, and Cherry & Pevsner as "Heavily modelled Italianate, but with French pavilion roofs, straddling the leafy cutting." The centre portion of the building was once a large waiting room and the left-hand pavilion the stationmaster's living accommodation.

The station was severely damaged by fire in 1980. Due to the efforts of the Camberwell Society, it was magnificently restored, with the right-hand pavilion as the new ticket office and the remainder converted to a public house called the Phoenix and Firkin (it rose again from the ashes). The station won a Civic Trust Award in 1986. The pub is currently run by O'Neill's.

At first, the two services calling here were: the South London Line (LBSCR) from London Bridge to Loughborough Park (later named East Brixton), extending to Victoria in 1867; and the High Level Crystal Palace Line (LCDR) from Ludgate Hill (now Blackfriars) to Crystal Palace via Nunhead, Honor Oak and Lordship Lane, until closure in 1954. The present service via the Catford Loop Line (Nunhead to Shortlands) opened in 1892.

Benecke's House, 174 Denmark Hill

86 **RUSKIN PARK:** In 1904, this area was to be sold for housing development; but the persistent efforts of Frank Trier (1853-1923) of 6 The Terrace, Champion Hill, persuaded the authorities to buy the site for a new park. Trier suggested the park be named after John Ruskin, who had been a local resident, and that donations might come from Ruskin's many admirers. Ruskin Park was opened by the LCC in 1907, following the purchase from Sir Robert Sanders MP (1867-1940) of eight large houses on Denmark Hill and the accompanying 24 acres (10 hectares) of gardens and fields. Financial support for the park came from the LCC and Lambeth, Camberwell and Southwark Metropolitan Borough Councils and the Metropolitan Public Gardens Association. A further 12 acres (5 hectares), formerly a market garden, became available in 1909 and opened in 1910. This is now the playing field between Finsen and Ferndene Roads.

The park was designed by Lt. Col. John James Sexby (1847-1924), who was responsible for many of the then new LCC parks, including Peckham Rye Park and Brockwell Park. One of the original houses served as the superintendent's home and for refreshments until the 1940s, when it was demolished.

A sundial was erected in the park to commemorate the visit of the composer Mendelssohn (1809-47) here in 1842. All that remains is the pedestal. It is on the site of 174 Denmark Hill, which was on the corner of Ferndene Road and Denmark Hill, the house of William and Henrietta Benecke, cousins of Mendelssohn's wife, Cécile. The sundial pedestal is of terracotta, decorated with Tudor roses; an inscription once recorded that Mendelssohn wrote his *Song without Words*, opus 62 no. 6 while staying here. Originally entitled *Camberwell Green*, the piece was later renamed *Spring Song*.

The Portico is all that remains of 'Woodlands', 170 Denmark Hill, a late 18th century house. When the house was demolished, the porch was kept and converted into a shelter, which now supports two large and aged wisterias. It was listed Grade II in 1951. An inscription, now gone, recorded that the house had been occupied 1799-1814 by a sea captain, James Wilson.

The management of Ruskin Park remained with the LCC until 1965, when it passed to the GLC, and then to Lambeth in 1970. In 1996, the Friends of Ruskin Park formed to encourage Lambeth Council to carry out repairs and maintenance and to promote enjoyment of the park. The attractive brick pergola (covered walkway) next to the bowling green was restored in 1999 due to their efforts; and with help from the Friends' Tree Fund 22 trees have been planted in three years. The wooden bandstand used to be a popular venue for Sunday afternoon concerts, but over the years it has fallen into disrepair; it is hoped that eventually it will be restored.

The *eastern* half of the park, which includes the former gardens to the original eight houses, is landscaped with a variety of fine, mature trees such as ash, lime, London plane, oak, maple, cedar, catalpa, poplar, purple beech and horse chestnut. Less common species are Caucasian wingnut, handkerchief (or dove) tree, maidenhair tree (ginkgo), black poplar, dawn redwood, sweetgum, tulip tree and contorted willow.

The *western* half of the park includes the playing field extension, which is bordered on all four sides by rows of ash trees. Parallel to the row of lime trees ran Dane Avenue, a road that linked Finsen and Ferndene Roads for a short period from 1907.

A suggested route is to enter by the lower Denmark Hill gate and proceed to the Portico, slip out to view **No. 87**, re-enter for sundial, pergola, bowling green, pond, bandstand and horse chestnut avenue. Note the magnificent 200 year old Turkey oak tree. Turn left uphill, passing the row of lime trees; *exit to Ferndene Road*.

87 TRADITIONAL RED GPO TELEPHONE BOX, Denmark Hill

SE5: Located outside Ruskin Park and opposite Champion Hill, this is a type K2, designed by Sir Giles Gilbert Scott and produced in 1927. It is made of cast iron and is slightly taller than the type K6 seen at North Dulwich Station. This was listed Grade II in 1987.

88 TEMPLE BOWLING CLUB, 1a Sunset Road SE5: Founded in

1881 by several local Camberwell businessmen, it was first located at 29½ Warner Road, now site of the Samuel Lewis Trust Buildings, built 1915 (at rear of Somerfield, Denmark Hill). The Club's name originated from William George Temple, the first treasurer. He was the licensee of the Golden Lion Public House and the famous Camberwell Palace of Varieties, now Butterfly Walk and Safeway.

In 1913 the Club moved to new premises on the site of what later became Rutland Court, 202 Denmark Hill. It moved again in 1931 to its present site in Sunset Road, sharing the grounds with the Sunset Lawn Tennis Club. The present pavilion and indoor facilities (and Rutland Court) were built in 1933.

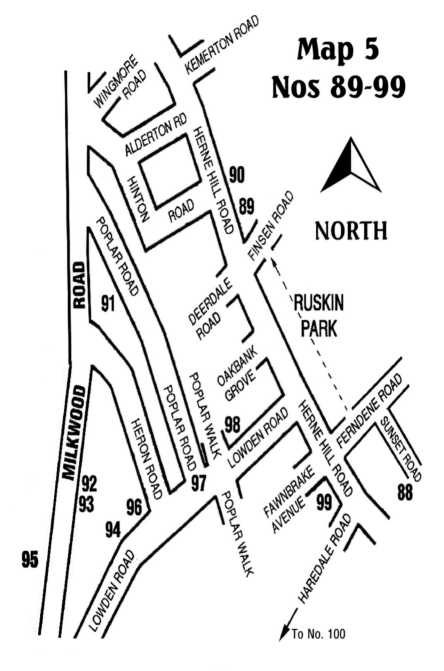

Map 5
Nos 89-99

NORTH

89 ST SAVIOUR'S PARISH HALL, Herne Hill Road:

This was built on a half-acre site, the land given by Sir Robert Sanders MP, later Baron Bayford. The building cost £5,000 and was paid for by a fund initiated in 1911 with parishioner contributions and profits from Choral Society concerts. Its red and brown brick contrasted with the grey stone church; it opened 7 February 1914.

The hall is a distinguished Arts & Crafts building by the architect Arthur Beresford Pite (1861-1934). Pite had worked on many projects with John Belcher from 1881-1900, and was Professor of Architecture at the Royal College of Art 1900-23. He would have known Herne Hill well. His father, Alfred Robert Pite (1832-1911) of the Habershon & Pite partnership, helped design the Milkwood Estate in the 1870s. Pite's brother, William Alfred Pite (1860-1949), designed King's College Hospital at Denmark Hill, which opened in 1913.

A club for the unemployed met in the parish hall during the 1930s depression. The Norwood Players staged plays here. The hall suffered slight air-raid damage in 1940. Services were held in the hall 'to beat the blackout' in 1942, and in 1950-51 following the breakdown of the church's heating system. In 1981 when the old church building was demolished, the stained glass windows were incorporated into the hall. The hall was listed Grade II in 1981, and is now used for all services and as an assembly hall for St Saviour's School.

90 ST SAVIOUR'S SCHOOL and site of CHURCH, Herne Hill Road:

The first school building was built in 1868 with stock bricks in Gothic style. It was built to serve the growing population in the newly built Herne Hill Road (north end), and Hinton, Hardess, Wanless and Wingmore Roads. The school was enlarged in 1892 and, according to directories of the time, was called 'St Saviour's Middle Class School for Girls & Infants'.

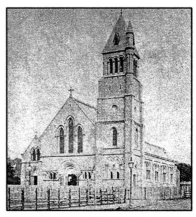

St. Saviour's Church in 1867

From c1920-c1950 it was 'St Saviour's School for Girls & Infants'. It has been a C of E primary school since the 1950s. The former church was built on land donated by James Lewis Minet (1807-85). The architect was A D Gough (1804-71). The church was consecrated 25 June 1867 and could hold over 900 people. It was built of ragstone dressed with Bath stone and had a tower. Pevsner described it in 1952 as "hearty, robust, and revolting". It was listed Grade II in 1955. The church and the neighbouring vicarage were demolished in April 1981, and services were transferred to the parish hall. The sites provided much needed school playgrounds.

91 MILKWOOD ESTATE bounded by Lowden, Milkwood and Poplar Roads, and including Heron and Jessop Roads: This 10 hectare (24 acre) development started in 1865, when the Suburban Village and General Dwelling Company applied for the lease. The company's aim was to build "healthy, pleasant and comfortable abodes for the overcrowded population of the metropolis," near to a railway station, and for each house to "contain from four to eight rooms with every domestic convenience." Unfortunately, by 1868 the Company Secretary had spent nearly all the funds and the shareholders refused to subscribe more money. The architects, Habershon & Pite, took over the project and reached an agreement with the freeholder, the Ecclesiastical Commissioners, to build between 480 and 650 dwellings. Lord Shaftesbury laid the first stone in 1869, and the estate was finished by the late 1870s. *The Builder* magazine reported in 1872 that the estate provided "a striking instance of the new neighbourhoods rising up...around the metropolis." Nevill's large model bakery, located between Milkwood and Heron Roads, was included in the scheme; and a number of houses were provided for the bakery workers.

92 HERNE HILL HARRIERS founded at 99 Milkwood Road: Now part of the Milkwood Open Space, No. 99 was a confectioner's shop owned by Mr & Mrs Robert Pickford in the late 1880s. The shop was demolished in the 1960s. A group of local boys used to meet in the front parlour of the shop; and to while away the long winter evenings, they formed a social club playing cards, dominoes and draughts. This led to the formation in 1889 of an athletics Club, the Herne Hill Harriers.

An early venue for committee meetings and social events was The Milkwood Tavern, which stood at the junction of Milkwood Road and Heron Road. Races would be organised around local roads. Cross-country events were held from The Pied Bull in Streatham. The track and field side of club activities were catered for by London County Grounds, now the Herne Hill Cycle Stadium at Burbage Road, which opened in 1892. The athletic (cinder) track at the Stadium was only four lanes wide; so for track and field events the club decided to

99 Milkwood Road (arrowed) shortly before demolition

leave Herne Hill in 1937 and use the newly built six lane track at Tooting Bec. They returned to the Herne Hill area in the 1970s for their cross-country training in Brockwell Park. Since their founding in 1889, nearly 100 club members have represented their country in athletics events.

93 MILKWOOD OPEN SPACE: Soon after Nevill's Bakery closed in the late 1960s, the building was demolished, together with some surrounding houses, to create the present Milkwood Road Open Space. More recently, concerned that the space had become run down and neglected, the Milkwood Residents' Association drew up plans and is now (2003) raising funds to convert the open space into a quality park with play and sports facilities.

94 JESSOP PRIMARY SCHOOL, Lowden Road: The school opened in 1876, named after Jessop Road. The present school building, put up in 1938, was enlarged in the 1960s and Jessop Road built over as a consequence. The school currently has about 250 pupils ranging in age from 3-11 years, including a nursery class providing pre-school places for between 25 and 50 pupils.

95 'THE MIRACLE OF HERNE HILL', 204 Milkwood Road: The site of 204 Milkwood Road is immediately opposite 169 Milkwood Road and near the Milkwood Open Space. The house was demolished in the 1960s. The 'miracle' is the story of Dorothy Kerin (1889-1963), who moved to No. 204 from Wandsworth in 1902 with her mother, following the death of her father. As a child, Dorothy suffered many years of serious and intractable illness. However, in February 1912, at a point when she had been pronounced on the verge of death, she made an immediate and unexplained recovery. This recovery, it is said, was accompanied by visions and the voices of angels singing that were heard throughout the house. A number of newspapers reported the story of this 'miracle'; as a result of extensive press coverage, Dorothy became famous. As well as continuing to hear voices and see visions, she later noted that stigmata appeared. She became well known as a healer and went on to found Burrswood, a Christian healing centre near Tunbridge Wells, still functioning today.

96 ST JOHN'S CHURCH, Lowden Road: This was built in 1881, designed by architects Horner & Waters as a mission church, affiliated to St Paul's Herne Hill, to minister to the growing population in the area. William Henry Stone Esq., 'Patron of the Parish of Herne Hill' and formerly of Casino House, laid the foundation stone. The church closed in 1988 and is now used as a community centre.

97 POPLAR ROAD/LOWDEN ROAD TRAMLINE TRACKS: It has been suggested that the two parallel lines still visible along the middle of Poplar Road are the remains of former tramlines. Road surfaces are not renewed as regularly on side-streets as on main roads; but the fact is that trams were all taken out of service by 1952! Note the particularly sharp right turn (Poplar Road to Lowden Road), where tram manoeuvres would have been fascinating to watch.

From 1884, a horse-drawn single-decker tram service ran from Camberwell to West Norwood, via Coldharbour Lane, Hinton Road and Milkwood Road with rearranged road level to Hinton Road under one railway bridge.

The LCC took over tram services in 1899 and, over time, introduced double-decker trams and electrification. However, Milkwood Road proved too narrow to take two lanes of the new style trams, and a detour had to be laid via Poplar Road and Lowden Road for the 'down' line track only. The 'up' track was laid along Milkwood Road. With the coming of London Passenger Transport Board in 1933, trams were gradually phased out and replaced with buses.

From the 1930s, the No. 48 tram ran from West Norwood along Norwood Road, Milkwood Road, Wanless Road, Herne Hill Road and Coldharbour Lane to Camberwell Green, Elephant & Castle and Bank.

No 48 Tram

98 ST PHILIP & ST JAMES CATHOLIC CHURCH, Poplar Walk:

Built in 1905 to the design of architect Francis William Tasker (1848-1904), at the corner with Lowden Road, it was one of a number of churches built from the bequest of Frances Elizabeth Ellis. The late Father Peter Clement (d 1999), parish priest from 1973-87, was in 1982 a founder member of the Herne Hill Society, which met in the church hall from 1982-92.

Map 6
Nos 100-120

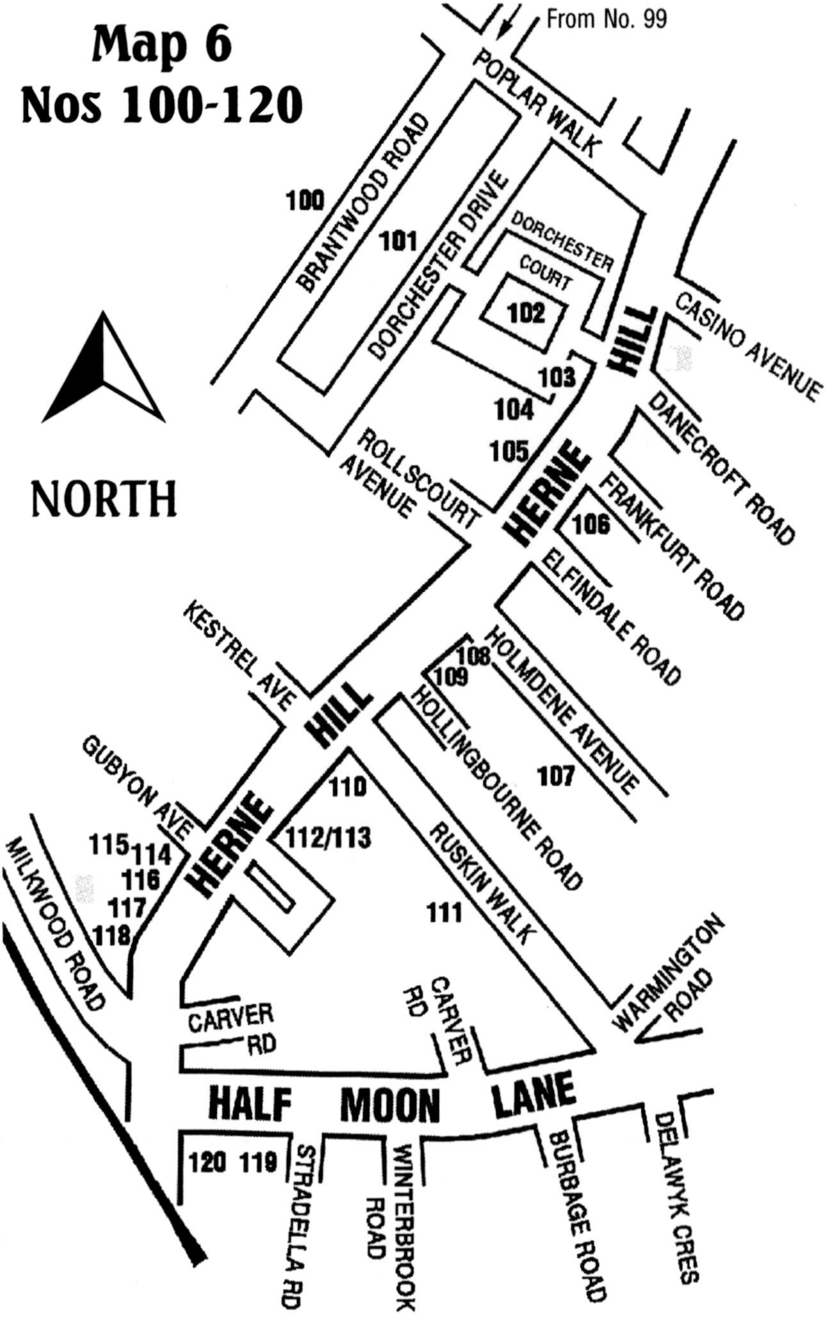

From No. 99

POPLAR WALK

BRANTWOOD ROAD

100

101

DORCHESTER DRIVE

DORCHESTER
COURT

102

103

104

105

HILL

CASINO AVENUE

DANECROFT ROAD

ROLLSCOURT AVENUE

HERNE

FRANKFURT ROAD

106

NORTH

ELFINDALE ROAD

KESTREL AVE

HOLMDENE AVENUE

108
109

107

HILL

HOLLINGBOURNE ROAD

110

GUBYON AVE

112/113

HERNE

RUSKIN WALK

115 114
116
117
118

MILKWOOD ROAD

111

WARMINGTON ROAD

CARVER
RD

CARVER RD

HALF   MOON   LANE

120 119

STRADELLA RD

WINTERBROOK ROAD

BURBAGE ROAD

DELAWYK CRES

Carnegie Library in 1906

99 CARNEGIE LIBRARY, 188 Herne Hill Road: The building was designed by Wakeford & Sons and built by Holliday & Greenwood in 1905. Opened to the public 9 July 1906, it was the first library to allow borrowers to browse amongst the shelves; this open access system was later adopted nation-wide.

Philanthropist Andrew Carnegie (1835-1919) supplied the £12,500 requested by the Borough of Lambeth to complete its library system by serving the Herne Hill area. Note the Lambeth coat of arms carved above the entrance and repeated in mosaic on the foyer floor. A plaque in the foyer with a relief of Carnegie commemorates his gift. A splendid example of Edwardian civic architecture, the building was listed Grade II in 1981. The outside walls and railings were separately listed Grade II the same year.

The library was threatened with closure in 1999; this initiated a campaign by the Friends of Carnegie Library to retain and revitalise it, attracting community support. Public rooms include main and children's libraries and an art gallery. Situated near Lambeth's boundary with Southwark, the library serves both boroughs.

100 BRANTWOOD ROAD: This is named after John Ruskin's home at Coniston in the Lake District. He purchased Brantwood in 1871 when he sold his Denmark Hill house, and lived there until he died in 1900. The road name was approved by the LCC in 1926.

101 DORCHESTER DRIVE: Built in 1936 by the developer Cyril Herbert Morell and possibly named after the Dorchester Hotel in Park Lane, which had opened in 1931. Each house is different, some having fine Art Deco interior features; distinctive 1930s features can be seen in some of the exteriors. The architects, Leslie H Kemp and Frederick E Tasker, were also working on a number of large cinemas at this time. Kemp later designed the Regal Cinema, which opened in 1940 in Camberwell Road; it is now a bingo hall. Tudor Stacks, a block of retirement flats, is built on the site of a house of the same name, which was once the home of a member of the Morell family.

102 DORCHESTER COURT, between Dorchester Drive and Herne Hill: Also built in 1936 by C H Morell and designed by architects Kemp and Tasker. There are eight blocks of flats built around a rectangular garden courtyard. Leslie H Kemp was a pioneer of District Heating (i.e. all flats heated from one boiler) and the system here operates from a detached boiler house with a tall chimney on the south side of the complex.

103 SITE of JOHN RUSKIN's HOUSE, 26 and 28 Herne Hill: The house was Georgian, semi-detached, three stories high plus an attic and a basement. The Ruskins moved here from Hunter Street, Brunswick Square in 1823. John got to know the then rural countryside of Dulwich and Norwood during his boyhood. In later years, he wrote about the neighbourhood he knew and loved, and criticised the late 19th century urbanisation of the area. In 1842, the Ruskins decided to move to a larger house in Denmark Hill, but they retained the lease of the Herne Hill house and let it out to a Miss Sarah Lee.

John Ruskin's House at 28 Herne Hill

In 1871, Ruskin moved from Denmark Hill to the Lake District, and gave the lease of the house as a wedding present to his cousin, Joan Agnew and her husband Joseph Arthur Severn (1842-1931), a watercolour artist. Ruskin often came back to stay with the Severns in the 1870s and 80s, using the house as a London base.

In 1883, the house was numbered as 28 Herne Hill; the Severns stayed until 1907. In 1909 a memorial plaque was placed on the house. However, as the house was demolished in 1923, the LCC erected a wooden post with a metal plaque in the front garden in 1925 as a replacement.

104 SITE of ANNA STORACE's HOUSE, Herne Hill Cottage (behind present 32 Herne Hill):

The exact location of this house is an educated guess, based on two different maps of the 1820s. Set back about 150m from the main road, it would have been approached by a path, now the driveway between The Quadrangle and the present 32 Herne Hill.

Anna Storace (pronounced Storachee; 1765-1817), the most accomplished opera singer of her day, lived here from 1809-17 after retiring from the stage. Born in London to an Italian father and an English mother, she studied singing in Italy, then moved to Vienna, where in 1784 Mozart cast her as his first Susanna in *The Marriage of Figaro*. Other major composers also created roles especially for her. After a disastrous marriage to John Abraham Fisher, she returned to England in 1787. By 1789 she was making regular appearances at Drury Lane, where her brother, Stephen Storace (1762-96), wrote many comic operas. Nancy, as she was known, topped the bill, unusually for a woman in London. In the 1790s she met the love of her life, John Braham (1773-1856), a tenor appearing with her at Drury Lane. They lived together and had a son; but about 1814 he left her for another woman. Six years after Anna's death, the Ruskins moved into their newly built house in front of her former home.

Anna's house may have been built as a cottage, but it is reputed that her friend and admirer Sir John Soane enlarged it into a three-storied residence with 12 fine rooms. By the 1860s it was known as Herne Hill Lodge, and later, The Lodge. It was demolished in the early 20th century, possibly as late as the 1930s when Dorchester Drive was built.

NB Another supposed site of Herne Hill Cottage is the former mansion called Matlock Manor at 18 Herne Hill, located on the south corner of Poplar Walk. This was demolished in the 1950s and is now occupied by a row of town houses.

105 THE QUADRANGLE, 34 Herne Hill: Two mock Jacobean
buildings sited opposite Carlton Parade shops on Herne Hill. They were built 1911-26 by the South London Provident Society, a charitable foundation, as homes for single women over 35. To be eligible as a tenant one had to be a civil servant, teacher, lecturer etc. or to have retired from the professions. It was a unique complex for the time and followed the development of Hampstead Garden Suburb, itself the first place to provide accommodation specifically for single working women. Twenty flats were built in 1911-12 facing Herne Hill, with a resident warden. The flat above the first archway was the visitors' room as no visitors were allowed into the flats. The warden would oversee, from her flat at No. 3, that this rule was obeyed. The flats had kitchens and toilets but no

bathrooms, as there were communal bathrooms and a laundry. Rents were nominal (initially, no rent was paid). In 1926, a further 16 flats were built on the site, larger but still without bathrooms. In 1960, the flats were modernised and made self-contained. The complex was sold in the 1980s and is no longer a charitable foundation.

106 CARLTON PARADE SHOPS, 63-77 Herne Hill: This row of

eight shops between Frankfurt and Elfindale Roads was built c1907 and named Carlton Parade after Carlton House, which used to stand nearby. The name Carlton Parade was dropped in 1913 when the present numbering was applied.

107 HOME of HENRY HAVELOCK ELLIS (1859-1939), 24

Holmdene Avenue: Physician and writer, Havelock Ellis travelled widely before studying medicine at St Thomas's Hospital. As a writer, his major work was the seven-volume *Studies in the Psychology of Sex*, written 1897-1928 and revised 1936. This work caused tremendous controversy and was banned in Britain. It was subsequently published in the USA and translated into many languages. He also wrote about Elizabethan and Jacobean theatre.

His wife Edith died in 1916. Subsequently he lived at 24 Holmdene Avenue; his name appears in the Electoral Registers for 1930-38. His autobiography was published posthumously in 1940.

108 HOME of MARIAN NOWAKOWSKI (1912-2000), 97 Herne

Hill: Born in Poland, he studied with the Polish bass, Adam Didur, at Lvóv Conservatory, before making his debut with the Lvóv Opera in 1937. After the Nazis' invasion of Poland he escaped to Britain and joined the émigré Polish army, based in Fife. He soon became a soloist with the newly formed Polish Army Choir giving concerts all over the country. After the war he was engaged as principal bass at Covent Garden and sang some 20 major roles 1947-63, notably Boris Godunov and the part of Sarastro in *The Magic Flute*. He also appeared at Sadler's Wells and in concert, opera and oratorio at the Albert Hall, around Britain and abroad. From 1964 he taught voice and opera production at the Royal College of Music in Kingston, Jamaica, where one of his pupils was Willard White. He also taught at the University of Southern Mississippi. In 1977 he returned to London, occasionally performing and teaching.

109 HOME of SIR RICHARD MUIR (1857-1924), 99 Herne Hill:

Muir was a prominent prosecuting barrister, and from about 1901 he was engaged in almost every Old Bailey trial of note until his death. His reputation was feared by many defendants and their counsel. His most famous case was the Crippen trial in 1910. Crippen murdered his actress wife and buried her dismembered body in the cellar of their Holloway home. He escaped on an Atlantic liner with his mistress, Ethel LeNeve, who was disguised as a boy. The captain of the liner wirelessed to Scotland Yard of Crippen's whereabouts, and Crippen was arrested in Quebec. At the trial, Muir interrogated Crippen for three hours, revealing his lies and evasions. The jury took 27 minutes to reach a verdict, and Crippen was later hanged at Pentonville prison.

Muir's secret was in the preparation of his cases. He would pore over his notes night after night until the case was foolproof. He was renowned for his meticulous precision and would place the evidence upon small cards, Muir's 'playing cards', as they came to be known.

Another well-known case, probably his most important, was that of Alfred and Albert Stratton, who were sentenced to death for the murder of Mr and Mrs Farrow at their chandler's store in Deptford in 1905. This was the first occasion that fingerprint evidence was used to obtain a conviction. Muir had studied the subject and knowledgeably questioned many expert witnesses.

Muir lived at 5 Cosbycote Avenue, Herne Hill from 1894-98. He moved to 99 Herne Hill (then numbered 15A) in 1898, when the house had just been built, living there until 1915. The house is now an osteopath's surgery, F W Bruggemeyer.

110 BOUNDARY POST, Ruskin Walk/Herne Hill: This post is

dated 1870 and marked the change in direction of the parish boundary between Camberwell and Lambeth. From this spot, the boundary came up Herne Hill and turned down Ruskin Walk. A smaller notice on the post denotes that the actual boundary was 25' (7.5m) away. The area south of Herne Hill (the road) between Ruskin Walk and Danecroft Road was in Lambeth; the boundaries changed in 1900. Similar posts along the old Camberwell boundary can be found in Elam Street and Champion Hill. Adjacent to the boundary post, there is a stone marked DULWICH MANOR, dated 1792 but recut in 1928. This marks the manorial boundary, which at this point is the same as the parish boundary. Similar stones are found in Champion Hill.

111 RUSKIN WALK, formerly

Simpson's Alley: This was once a footpath connecting Herne Hill with Half Moon Lane. It came to be called Simpson's Alley in honour of Thomas and Sarah Simpson of Herne Hill, who had donated land for St Jude's School and for St Paul's Church. Made up into a street, with its first houses built c1905, it was renamed in memory of John Ruskin, who used to follow it en route to Croxted Lane and Dulwich. Richard Church sorrowfully recalled the felling of aspens in 1910-11 "preparatory to widening the walk into a suburban road" with foundations for further houses. *John Ruskin aged 24*

112 ST PAUL'S CHURCH, Herne Hill: The church was originally

designed by George Alexander in Early English style, and built at a cost of £6,707 raised by subscription. The leasehold land was given by Mrs Sarah Simpson (1761-1847), and the freehold was negotiated from the DCE. The church was consecrated 21 December 1844. In February 1858, it was destroyed by fire, leaving only the tower, spire and outer walls remaining. The Rev. Matthew Anderson (1799-1893, vicar 1844-69) had the prudence and foresight to insure the church building for the sum of £3,500 from his own pocket. Holland & Hannen rebuilt it to the design of George Edmund Street (1824-81), who later designed the Law Courts in the Strand. The building cost £5,200 excluding the windows, which were all donated. The church reopened on 21 October 1858 and could accommodate 700 people. The carvings are by Thomas Earp (1828-93), the glass

St. Paul's Church in 1844

by Hardman and the organ was built by Holditch. John Ruskin called the new church "one of the loveliest in the country and one that makes the fire a matter of rejoicing". There is a memorial to Ruskin on the north wall of the nave, unveiled in 1901 by the Pre-Raphaelite painter, William Holman Hunt (1827-1910).

The rood screen is a memorial to the dead of WW1 and was dedicated in March 1921. WW2 bombing in 1940 damaged the roof and pews. A near-miss V I bomb in 1944 destroyed nearly all the glass, leaving only two complete windows remaining: one depicting St Peter, west of the south aisle; the other of St John, west of the north aisle. Of the modern windows, the East window glass is by Lillian J Pollack (1949). St Paul's was listed Grade II* in 1954.

113 **THE OLD VICARAGE, St Paul's Church, Herne Hill:** This Grade II listed building was designed in High Gothic style by architect Richard William Drew and built c1866 by Buck & Norwood. The cost was £2,300, of which £1,000 was borrowed from Queen Anne's Bounty Fund. A new vicarage was built at 8 Ruskin Walk in 1976; since 1977 the old vicarage has been a private nursery and pre-prep school.

114 **HERNE HILL MANSIONS, 110-112 Herne Hill:** This block of 16 purpose-built flats was built 1898-1900 on the site of The Abbey, or Herne Hill Abbey, a large early 19th century mansion. Also built on the site are Abbey Mansions, 351-381 Milkwood Road and Herne Hill Station. There is no obvious reason why the house was called The Abbey or to link it with any religious foundation. It was probably built in Gothic-Revival style. From 1883-98, The Abbey was 70 Herne Hill.

Thomas Vyse (1782-1861), a prosperous straw-hat manufacturer, lived at The Abbey from the 1840s until his death. His business, Vyse and Son Ltd., was located in the Wood Street area of the City of London and survived until 1961. He was one of the subscribers to the building of the first St Paul's Church in 1844.

115 ABBEY MANSIONS, HOME of BRANSBY WILLIAMS, Milkwood Road: This block of four purpose-built flats, built c1900, can be reached via the petrol station and the path alongside 381 Milkwood Road.

The actor and music hall artist, Bransby Williams (1870-1961, real name Pharez), had his address at Flat 1 from the 1940s until his death. He did character impersonations of leading actors and music hall comedians and specialised in musical monologues and the portrayal of characters from Dickens and Shakespeare. His famous recitations included 'The Green Eye of the Little Yellow God' and 'The Pigtail of Li Fan Fu'.

Memorial Plaque, Herne Hill Sorting Office

116 SORTING OFFICE, 130 Herne Hill: The Sorting Office, or 'Postmens Office', originally located at No. 134, moved to its present premises at No. 130 about 1917. A memorial plaque in the lobby honours colleagues who died in WW1.

117 Former LCC FIRE BRIGADE STATION, 132 Herne Hill:

Built for the LCC Fire Brigade Committee in 1905-6, it was staffed by a Station Officer, five firemen and a coachman, who lived in the flats above the station. A pair of horses to pull the fire engine was stabled on the site of the present petrol station; and a third horse, possibly a shire, was used to help pull coaches in difficulty up Herne Hill.

The Fire Brigade generally operated a continuous duty system until 1920, when the two-shift system was introduced. This, together with the introduction of motor-driven appliances, made for a much more efficient service. Nevertheless, the Fire Station closed in 1920, for economic reasons. In recent years, the ground floor has been used as a car showroom and a furniture shop. Sainsbury's Local opened in March 2003.

118 POST OFFICE, 134 Herne Hill: From 1917, No. 134 was

used as a shop; in 1938 it became the main Post Office. Before 1938, Herne Hill was served by a number of sub-post offices, the principal one being at 25 Half Moon Lane, where Mrs Elizabeth King ran a fancy stationers and post office from 1903, when the shops known as 'The Parade' were built. There is still a post-box outside the shop.

Most of the other sub-post offices in SE24 have gone: 21 Rymer Street, off Railton Road, closed c1937 and is now a shop; 75 Milkwood Road closed in 1967 and was demolished; 65 Herne Hill closed in 1969 and is now an estate agent; 123 Norwood Road closed in 1972 and is now a flat.

119 SHOPS, 12-24 Half Moon Lane: These shops between the

Half Moon pub and Stradella Road were built c1896 to help serve the growing population in the streets to the north and east; they were called 'Springfield Parade' after the former mansion on the site of the present Stradella/Winterbrook Roads.

No. 16 was a provisions store, David Greig, from 1910; note the 'DG' logo under the window. The actor Michael Crawford (b 1942) spent part of his childhood in the flat above this shop, where his stepfather was manager. The family then moved to Winterbrook Road, where Michael remained to age 21. The David Greig chain of shops ceased trading c1977. No. 24 was a draper's shop until 1927, when Lloyds Bank took over the premises.

Half Moon Public House c1880

120 HALF MOON PUBLIC HOUSE, 10 Half Moon Lane: There has been an inn on this site since the 17th century; the present building, dating from 1896, is the third. Now listed Grade II*, it was designed by architect James William Brooker (c1852-1904) in 'Jacobeathan Revival' style. There are three bars, including a small wine bar (snug bar) which is lined with six painted mirrors by Walter Gibbs & Sons of Blackfriars Road. The screen windows around the saloon bar are cut glass, possibly also by Gibbs, with each window having a central engraved flower design. Gibbs's work is highly regarded; and although Walter Gibbs had died in 1889, his widow, Sarah, and sons, Walter and Horace, successfully carried on the business until the 1930s.

In the 19th century, the pub was noted for its flower gardens, lawns and tea gardens; also, quoits and bowls were played. The Herne Hill and Dulwich Social Club used to meet here in the 1870s. It is said that a former manager had been chauffeur to Frank Sinatra. Musicians who played here and went on to become famous include Eric Clapton (in the 1970s) and the Irish band U2; and the tradition of live entertainment continues to this day.

SOURCES
Books:

ALDRICH, Megan (editor) *The Craces, Royal Decorators 1768-1899* (1990)

BLANCHE, W H *The Parish of Camberwell* (1875)

BOAST, Mary *The Story of Dulwich* (1990)

BOAST, Mary *The Story of Camberwell* (1996)

BOOTH, Catherine Branwell *Catherine Booth* (1972)

CHERRY, Bridget & PEVSNER, Niklaus *The Buildings of England: London 2, South* (1983)

CHURCH, Richard *The Golden Sovereign* (1957)

CONNELL, Rev. J C *Herne Hill Baptist Church: These Fifty Years* (1949)

COOK, Eric T *St Saviour's Herne Hill, The Story of 100 Years 1867-1967* (1967)

COULTER, John *Norwood Past* (1996)

CRAWFORD, Michael *Parcel Arrived Safely: Tied With String* (1999)

DARBY, Patrick *Kingswood, A History of the House and Estate* (1999)

DEARDEN, James S *John Ruskin, An Illustrated Life 1819-1900* (1981)

DEARDEN, James S *John Ruskin's Camberwell* (1990)

DIXON, Ken *Brixton Town Trails* (1990)

DIXON, Ken *Effra: Lambeth's Underground River* (1993)

DRAPER, Marie P G *Lambeth Open Spaces, An Historical Account* (1979)

DUDMAN, Jill *Brixton and Norwood in Old Photographs* (1995)

DULWICH PICTURE GALLERY *Charles Barry, Junior and the Dulwich College Estate* (1986)

DYOS, H J *Victorian Suburb* (1961)

EDWARDS, Rhoda *Lambeth Stoneware* (1973)

ELLIS, Havelock *My Life* (1940; 1967 ed.)

ERNEST, Johanna *The Life of Dorothy Kerin* (1983)

FELSTEAD, Sidney Theodore *Sir Richard Muir - a memoir of a public prosecutor* (1927)

GALER, Alan M *Norwood & Dulwich: Past and Present* (1890)

GIROUARD, Mark *Victorian Pubs* (1984)

GRAY, A. Stuart *Edwardian Architecture* (1985)

GREEN, Brian *Around Dulwich* (1982)

GREEN, Brian *Victorian & Edwardian Dulwich* (1988)

GREEN, Brian *The Home Front 1939-45* (1995)

HARLEY, Robert J *Camberwell & West Norwood Tramways* (1993)

HUMPHREY, Stephen *Britain in old Photographs: Camberwell, Dulwich & Peckham* (1996)

JAMES, Robert Rhodes *Henry Wellcome* (1994)

JENKYNS, Patricia M *The Story of Sir Henry Bessemer* (1984)

JENKYNS, Patricia M *A Glance at the History of Herne Hill* (1992)

LEES, L E S *The Story of St Paul's Church 1844-1944* (1944)

LOCKETT, Richard *Samuel Prout (1783-1852)* (1985)

LCC *Replanning London Schools* (1947)

LCC *Names of Streets and Places in the Administrative County of London* (1955)

MITCHELL, Vic & SMITH, Keith *Victoria to Bromley South* (1992)

MITCHELL, Vic & SMITH, Keith *South London Line, London Bridge to Victoria* (1995)

PEVSNER, Niklaus *The Buildings of England: London Volume 2* (1952)

PIPER, Alan *A History of Brixton* (1996)

RUSKIN, John *Modern Painters* (1843-1860)

RUSKIN, John *Praeterita (1885)*

SERVICE, Alastair (editor) *Edwardian Architecture and its origins* (1975)

SUMMERSON, John *Georgian London* (1969)

SURVEY of LONDON, *vol. 26 St. Mary Lambeth, Southern Area* (1956)

THE THIRTIES SOCIETY *Farewell My Lido* (1991)

VAN ASH, C & SAX ROHMER, E *Master of Villainy* (1972)

VAN DEN BERGH, Tony *Who Killed Freddie Mills?* (1991)

WILSON, J B *The Story of Norwood* (1990)

WOOLACOTT, Ron *Nunhead Notables* (2002)

Other Publications:

ARCHITECTURAL DESIGN, vol. 49 no. 10-11, 1979
> *Britain in the Thirties, Giles Gilbert Scott*, by Gavin Stamp

A Brief History of St Paul's Church Herne Hill, by Peter L Baldwin (1996)

THE BUILDER, 7 March, 1958, p. 439
> *St Faith's Church*

FRIENDS OF WEST NORWOOD CEMETARY, newsletter 31, January 1998, pages 7-10
> *Sir Richard David Muir*, by Paul Graham

GODFREY EDITION Old Ordnance Survey Maps: -
> Brixton & Herne Hill 1870 (Bill Marshall)
> Brixton & Herne Hill 1894 (Alan Godfrey)
> Streatham Hill & Tulse Hill 1870 (Bill Marshall)
> Streatham Hill & Tulse Hill 1894 (W W Marshall)

HERNE HILL SOCIETY, newsletters 1982-2002, particularly:
> No 11, November 1984, p 6, 7, 10, Railton Road Methodist Church, by Frank Nash
> No 35, January 1991, p 6, 7, Charles Woolley (1846-1922)
> No 69, Winter 1999/2000, p 8, Howletts Acre, by Jeffrey Segal

STANFORD'S Library Map of London and its Suburbs (1862)

TURNER STUDIES, HIS ART & EPOCH 1775-1851 (1987)
> *The Turner Collector: Elhanan Bicknell,* by Peter Bicknell

INDEX